About this book

The George W. Bush administration maintains that in sub-Saharan Africa it is making major new contributions in fighting disease, promoting development, fostering democracy, and promoting peace. Yet, despite the rhetoric, is the Bush administration really working to bring about a fairer and more just Africa?

Though aid has increased and a major AIDS initiative has been launched, Copson argues that US policy in Africa falls well short of meeting reasonable standards of fairness or justice. Foreign aid is losing its focus on development as political priorities come to the fore, US barriers to African exports remain substantial, and the AIDS program is in danger of flagging due to unilateralism and ideological controversy. An increasingly military approach to fighting the 'Global War on Terror' in Africa and securing energy imports carries serious risks for the region. Copson concludes by assessing the prospects of a more equitable policy emerging in future administrations.

About the author

Raymond W. Copson is an independent scholar specializing in African affairs and US relations with Africa. He teaches at the Johns Hopkins University School of Advanced International Studies and at the George Washington University's Elliott School of International Affairs. Copson is editor of the Online Africa Policy Forum at the Center for Strategic and International Studies. Until 2005, he worked at the Congressional Research Service of the US Library of Congress. He has previously lectured in international relations at the University of Nairobi, Kenya, and the University of Ibadan, Nigeria.

RAYMOND W. COPSON

The United States in Africa

Bush policy and beyond

Zed Books
LONDON | NEW YORK

David Philip
CAPE TOWN

in association with

International African Institute
Royal African Society
Social Science Research Council

The United States in Africa: Bush policy and beyond was first published in association with the International African Institute, the Royal African Society and the Social Science Research Council in 2007 by

in Southern Africa: David Philip (an imprint of New Africa Books)
99 Garfield Road, Claremont 7700, South Africa

in the rest of the world: Zed Books Ltd, 7 Cynthia Street, London N1 9JF, UK and Room 400, 175 Fifth Avenue, New York, NY 10010, USA

www.zedbooks.co.uk
www.iaionthe.net
www.royalafricansociety.org
www.ssrc.org

Cover designed by Andrew Corbett
Set in Arnhem and Futura Bold by Ewan Smith, London
index: <ed.emery@thefreeuniversity.net>
Printed and bound in Malta by Gutenberg Press Ltd

Distributed in the USA exclusively by Palgrave Macmillan, a division of St Martin's Press, LLC, 175 Fifth Avenue, New York, NY 10010.

A catalogue record for this book is available from the British Library
US CIP data are available from the Library of Congress

ISBN 978 1 84277 914 9 hb
ISBN 978 1 84277 915 6 pb

Contents

1 | Introduction

Does the United States have a policy toward sub-Saharan Africa that is fair and just? What could be done to change policy in ways that would make it fairer and more just? These are the underlying questions that have inspired this short volume.

Many Bush administration[1] critics might find the first question absurd on its face. Their heartfelt opposition to US policies on Iraq, the Israel–Palestine dispute, global warming, the International Criminal Court, and other issues inevitably creates a predisposition to doubt that the administration could or would pursue a just and fair policy in Africa. Key features of Africa policy, such as the administration's long delay in mounting a meaningful response to the crisis in Darfur, US aid to warlords in Somalia, and the seeming US endorsement of the oppressive Obiang regime in oil-rich Equatorial Guinea only serve to affirm their doubts. But the issue is not so simple. Under President Bush, US economic assistance to sub-Saharan Africa has reached record levels; a large program has been launched to fight the African AIDS pandemic; and through a strategic commitment of diplomatic resources, the administration made a major contribution to ending the civil war in southern Sudan.

This volume will acknowledge these positive features of the Bush administration's Africa policy, which have been inspired in part by the President's response to his base in the evangelical Christian community, and in part by political pressures coming from other groups that have long sought a better future for Africa. At the same time, these steps toward a fairer and more just Africa policy have been undercut by the strong element of political realism that has always affected US policy toward the sub-Saharan region, by the influence of neoconservatives and other ideologues, and by economic self-interest.

According to the White House, the intention of the Bush administration is to 'work with others for an African continent that lives in liberty, peace, and growing prosperity,' but in fact, policy is falling far short of this vision – both in terms of working with others and in terms of advancing what the White House says is a 'core value' of the United States: 'preserving human dignity.'[2] In recent years, policy has come to be more and more influenced by two security interests, the Global War on Terror (GWOT) and the protection of oil supplies, that are pushing the United States away from a fairer and more just relationship with Africa. These security interests are real, but are not so great or compelling in the sub-Saharan region that they should be allowed to overwhelm the better aspects of policy. A particular danger is that the pursuit of GWOT in the Islamic parts of Africa, combined with the unpopularity among Muslims of US policies in the Middle East, could provoke regional conflict and instability – as well as lasting alienation from the United States.

Fairness and justice in Africa policy

A concern with justice and fairness in a book about foreign policy might seem misplaced to some readers, particularly those raised in the realist school of analysis, discussed below. It is the author's conviction, however, that justice and fairness should always be major considerations in policy toward any region, on both moral and practical grounds. Whether one accepts the moral argument – that the United States ought to pursue justice and fairness in its relations with all countries – is a matter of personal belief. The fact that the United States has lost influence in the world under the Bush administration because it has been perceived as unfair and unjust in its foreign policy should, however, be of practical concern to all. If policymakers lose sight of the importance for the United States of being regarded as a fair and just actor on the international stage, they are not likely to be able to protect US security interests in Africa or elsewhere.

The moral argument for a fair and just policy in sub-Saharan Africa is particularly compelling because the United States has incurred moral obligations toward the region over a troubling history of more than three centuries. Although it may be that the European colonizers bear a heavier responsibility for the problems Africa faces today, the truth is that the United States must share a considerable portion of the blame. Slaves brought by force from Africa, and their descendants who continued to live in slavery until the American Civil War (1861–65), were central to the economic development of the American South and the country as a whole. The injustices meted out to America's Africa-descended population have never been fully expiated, nor even ended. In Africa, the slave trade brought only turmoil, conflict, and impoverishment. The importation of slaves to the United States became illegal from 1808, but many were smuggled in on the eve of the Civil War as southern extremists agitated for legalizing the trade once again. The participation of Americans in the international slave trade was also made illegal and punishable by death in the early nineteenth century, but these laws were poorly enforced. American captains and crews were enthusiastic participants in the export of many thousands from West Africa to Cuba and Brazil through much of the nineteenth century, and no one was hanged for the crime until 1862, after President Lincoln had taken office.[3] In that same century, Liberia was launched by well-to-do Americans, some motivated by humanitarian considerations but many others by a concern to cleanse the United States of free blacks regarded as unassimilable and a threat to plantation society in the American South. In subsequent decades, this American offshoot was sadly neglected; and in the late twentieth century, when Liberia had fallen into its time of troubles, US forces time and again stood offshore during violent upheavals, or intervened solely to rescue Americans and other foreigners – while the people of Liberia were left to suffer.

Liberia, of course, was by no means the only instance in the twentieth century in which the United States failed to act justly in its relations with Africa. The procrastination, delay, and absence of US leadership during the 1994 genocide in Rwanda is perhaps the most painful disappointment in recent memory, but there are many others. President Lyndon Johnson's refusal to back deployment of a United Nations peacekeeping force in Rhodesia, after the white minority regime issued its Unilateral Declaration of Independence from Britain in 1965, comes to mind. So does South Africa policy during the Reagan administration, when, rather than standing forthrightly for democracy and human rights, the United States temporized with the apartheid regime under a policy of 'constructive engagement.'

There have been bright spots in US relations with Africa, of course, but on balance these do not make up for the damage done over the years. President Carter worked diligently in support of the negotiations that brought an end to the Rhodesian conflict and ushered Zimbabwe to independence in 1980.[4] In 1985, Congress passed a major African famine relief bill and provided hundreds of millions of dollars in emergency aid.[5] The next year saw Congress enact sweeping sanctions against South Africa over President Reagan's veto.[6] The Clinton administration – belatedly to be sure, as was the case with other governments – came to recognize the danger that the AIDS pandemic posed to Africa's future, and Vice-President Al Gore mobilized new funds from several agencies to fight the disease.

Despite the occasional good things that happen in US Africa policy, however, an overall sense of disappointment prevails among those who hope for a better future for the region. In case after case over the years, the United States has done less than it could to fight poverty, foster peace, and promote human rights in Africa; even though policymakers in every administration have expressed their commitment to attaining these very goals. Creating a better future for Africa is not the responsibility of the United States alone, of course. Other donor governments, international organizations, non-governmental organizations, and African leaders themselves all have great responsibilities in this difficult time for the region. But the United States has its own special obligations in sub-Saharan Africa and should act accordingly. As a world leader, it also has a special responsibility to inspire other wealthy countries to fulfill their own responsibilities toward the region.

What would be the principal characteristics of a fair and just policy toward sub-Saharan Africa? These may seem obvious, but are worth reviewing here for the sake of clarity. 'First, do no harm,' the guideline for physicians attributed to Hippocrates, should be the overarching concern for policymakers, such as those in the Department of Defense who are now busily expanding the US military role across the Sahel and Sahara. Second, the protection of the poor, the neglected, and women and children is the hallmark of any ethical system worthy of respect, and must also be at the heart of just and fair policy toward Africa. Efforts to promote economic opportunity, healthcare, and education are key to helping the poor, as is the removal of economic barriers (including trade barriers!) that take away their hope of a better life. Third, support for civil liberties and freedom of expression should be part of a just policy toward Africa; and, finally, such a policy must promote peace and encourage peacemakers.

Realism and neoconservatism in Africa policy

A key to understanding the limitations of US Africa policy across all the post-World War II administrations is to recognize that professional policymakers have consistently been drawn from the 'realist' school of international relations theory. In the realist view, Africa has little to offer the United States; and events in Africa rarely threaten the United States in any significant way – hence there is little reason to be involved there. The realist approach to foreign policy is imbibed by rising diplomats and policymakers in the international relations programs of the major universities and mainstream American think tanks. Henry Kissinger, National Security Advisor and then Secretary of State in the Nixon and Ford administrations, and Zbigniew Brzezinski, President Carter's National Security Advisor, exemplify the type. Those who take a more idealistic approach to foreign affairs tend not to reach the corridors of power in the executive branch, but rather find themselves in academic positions or working in non-governmental organizations.

A realist pursues the national interest narrowly defined – 'interest defined in terms of power,' in the words of Hans Morgenthau, pioneer theorist in the realist school.[7] Defining power, measuring power, and discerning which alternative policies will most effectively promote power have always been subjects of debate among realists, but there has been a general consensus among most realists most of the time that Africa has little relevance to US power. Realists see themselves as prudent and pragmatic; and prudent, pragmatic US policymakers have tended to devote their time, energies, and US resources to other regions and other priorities they see as central to preserving national security or advancing US power.

In the past, cold war pressures occasionally persuaded realists to intervene in African affairs. In 1960, for example, the United States plotted to assassinate Congo's prime minister Patrice Lumumba, viewed as a Soviet ally,[8] and Kissinger channeled aid to rebel groups in Angola in the mid-1970s to counter Soviet and later Cuban support for the government. Congress put a stop to Kissinger's interference in Angola, but aid to Angolan rebels resumed in the Reagan years. Brzezinski was deeply concerned by Soviet and Cuban support for Ethiopia during the 1977–78 'Ogaden crisis,' moving ships toward the region and forging an alliance with the Siad Barre government in Somalia. But these were episodes in the global cold war chess game rather than part of a coherent, long-term policy based on a view that Africa was in itself important to the United States. In the 1990s, with the end of the rivalry between the United States and the Soviet Union in Africa, US aid to Africa declined sharply. Only at the end of the decade, as public pressure for a US response to the AIDS pandemic and Africa's complex humanitarian emergencies mounted, did assistance levels begin to recover.

During the 2000 campaign, candidate George W. Bush seemed to place himself squarely in the realist school in his thinking about Africa, stating in the second presidential debate that Africa is an 'important continent. But there's got to be priorities, and the Middle East is a priority for a lot of reasons, as is Europe and the Far East, our own hemisphere. And those are my four top priorities should I be the president.'[9] Subsequent chapters will show that the realist thinking reflected in this statement has remained influential and continues to restrain the level of US engagement with Africa, despite the President's AIDS initiative and some other positive developments. Some realists today, both in and out of government, are beginning to pay more attention to Africa because of its growing importance as a supplier in global energy markets. The impact of this attention, however, has not been favorable for Africa, since it has been reflected in a noticeable tendency among policymakers to overlook – or pay minimal attention to – human rights violations and corruption in Africa's oil-rich countries.

The Bush administration has been noteworthy for the rise of 'neoconservatives' to positions of influence over foreign policy. Because of their emphases on pre-emptive intervention before threats have materialized, on transforming Middle East politics, and on using force to project American values, they have been soundly criticized by classical realists, who place such a high value on prudence and pragmatism.[10] Like the realists, however, neoconservatives have generally taken little interest in Africa – although their enthusiasm for waging the Global War on Terror is reflected in the worrisome Trans Sahara Counterterrorism Initiative (TSCTI), aimed at preventing the emergence of 'new Afghanistans' in Africa and in moves to create a new Africa Command in the Defense Department. In theory, this program is to have a substantial economic development component, but economic assistance funds are in short supply and the military component threatens to grow disproportionately large. The neoconservative influence is also seen in the assistance given by the United States to warlords in Somalia in 2006 and the subsequent support for Ethiopia's ouster of the Islamic Courts Union from Mogadishu, Kismayo, and other positions. These issues are discussed in a later chapter. As is the case among realists, moreover, some neoconservatives are increasingly interested in African oil. They highlight its growing importance as a way of winning support for greater military involvement in the region.

The idealist influence in Africa policy

While the realist influence has been dominant in Africa policy over the years, realists have never held complete sway. Indeed, fairly often, idealistic forces coming from outside the realist consensus have intervened to send Africa policy in unexpected directions. These directions have sometimes led to the brighter moments in US relations with Africa, such as the African famine relief and anti-apartheid legislation noted above. When this happens, realist policymakers may be forced to accept policy change in directions favored by idealists, and even to adopt the language of the idealists. Official policy statements may, in deference to the pressures from idealists, come to express commitments to preventing genocide, ending hunger,[11] or resolving African conflicts, but the actions and resources ultimately devoted to these objectives typically fall short of the need. Realists always push back against the idealistic impulse, trying to force Africa policy to return to its minimalist core so that they can maximize resources for other regions and other priorities. As a result, US economic assistance resources are consistently constrained despite the repeated announcement of Africa aid initiatives to prevent famine, improve education, promote the use of the Internet, reduce malaria's toll, or achieve other worthy objectives. Peacekeeping operations, initially endorsed by US policymakers, are rarely given the resources needed to do their jobs with full effect.

Yet, Africa policy does not spring fully formed from the Department of State, where realists predominate; nor from the White House's National Security Council or the Department of Defense, with their mix of realists and neoconservatives. Rather, it results from a surprisingly lively and contentious Africa policymaking process in Washington and beyond, which allows idealists and others to have an impact. Representatives of advocacy and nongovernmental organizations; think-tank experts; members of Congress – as well as their personal and committee staff; personnel from executive branch agencies; and lobbyists of various sorts engage in a continuous round of discussions and debates that affect Africa policy. Through much of the year, hearings, speeches, panel discussions, and other Africa-related events occur on nearly a daily basis in Washington itself, while Africa events are also taking place on college campuses, in churches, and elsewhere around the country. All of this happens because individuals as well as a host of grassroots and nationwide organizations are concerned about Africa and its future, want their voices to be heard, and expect a response from their government.

Sometimes it seems that US presidents themselves come at

Africa policy from outside the realist consensus, from personal conviction and because they are politicians, aware of the sympathies and concerns of the public and key constituencies. Jimmy Carter was the first president to devote a trip exclusively to Africa, and his activism in resolving the Rhodesia conflict has already been noted. These Africa interests later blossomed into a post-presidential career dedicated in significant measure to promoting human rights, free elections, and improved living standards around the region. President George H. W. Bush, father of George W. Bush, sent US armed forces into Somalia in December 1992 to combat famine, contrary to any realist notion of prudence or pursuit of the national interest narrowly defined.[12] Public and congressional pressure for a response, inspired by harrowing media coverage of the suffering of Somalis, was certainly intense. But the deployment came after Bush had already lost his bid for a second term, and he could easily have left the problem to his successor, Bill Clinton. There is a literature that attributes the Somalia operation, which was authorized by a UN Security Council resolution,[13] to a supposed US interest in Somalia as a potential oil producer,[14] but this thesis ignores the tremendous concern in the United States over the humanitarian situation in Somalia at the time. The US action did not end well – the killing of eighteen US servicemen in Mogadishu in October 1993 entrenched an aversion to the deployment of US troops in Africa that remains influential to this day. Nonetheless, thousands of Somali lives were probably saved.[15]

George W. Bush reportedly told confidants on several occasions that he believed God had called him to seek the presidency and that he had a mission to perform in that office.[16] The potential consequences of this sense of calling or mission are frightening when it comes to Middle East policy, Iran, or other issues with a military dimension; but it may have worked to Africa's benefit by influencing the creation of PEPFAR, as the chapter on AIDS policy will show. The AIDS chapter will also note that some observers attribute PEPFAR to the influence in the White House of Michael Gerson, a persuasive evangelical Christian and speechwriter to the President.[17] Gerson left the administration in June 2006, and this may tend to lessen the impact of idealism on administration Africa policy. Moreover, to the extent that the President propelled the United States into an ill-advised and disproportionate war with 'radical Islam' or 'Islamic fascists' – a phrase used by the President himself[18] – Africa may suffer.

Presidential attention to Africa is usually fleeting, and the more typical pattern is for idealistic forces to influence Africa policy through Congress, which because of its powers of oversight and law-making can shift the direction of policy or even compel policy changes. Congress may be energized by public pressures that in turn are aroused by a humanitarian crisis or injustice in Africa as a result of media exposure and campaigns by advocacy organizations. This pattern was seen in the US response to the Sahel famines of the 1970s and mid-1980s, or in passage of the 1986 anti-apartheid legislation, which followed years of campus demonstrations, sit-ins and arrests, candlelight vigils at the South African embassy, and other protests. Today, congressional pressures inspired by the Save Darfur campaign and other idealists are helping to keep the Darfur crisis on the administration's foreign policy agenda. Congress can also affect Africa policy in non-crisis situations. For example, advocacy groups working with concerned members over the years have helped to assure that US foreign assistance policies pay at least some attention to the needs of the poor and the hungry; foster micro-enterprise; and fight malaria, tuberculosis, and other diseases in addition to AIDS.

The media and media personalities play a vital role in pushing Africa policy in a more idealistic direction. The Darfur crisis has received extensive coverage in the press and Nicholas Kristof's

New York Times editorial columns on the situation were awarded a Pulitzer Prize in April 2006. In May 2006, Oprah Winfrey, whose daytime television show has an average daily audience of 49 million people, hosted an appearance by Liberia's President Ellen Johnson-Sirleaf, bringing unprecedented public attention to a country with historic US links, noted above, that have been too often ignored or forgotten.[19] The Irish rock star Bono has had an immense impact with the American public and Congress on African issues, particularly AIDS, debt, and foreign assistance levels. Other stars, including Angelina Jolie, Brad Pitt, and Denzel Washington, have also worked hard to call attention to Africa's problems and needs.

The number of organizations involved in Africa policy advocacy from an idealist perspective is quite remarkable. Many have mandates that extend beyond Africa, but are frequently involved in African issues. These include Amnesty International, Human Rights Watch, Bread for the World, Physicians for Human Rights, and others. Some have an Africa-specific focus, such as Debt, AIDS, Trade, and Africa (DATA), which has Bono as spokesman; Africa Action, based on Capitol Hill; the Advocacy Network for Africa (ADNA); and Africare, an African-American organization. Church-based groups have been influential for years, among them the Africa Faith and Justice Network, a Catholic organization; Catholic Relief Services; Church World Service; the American Friends Service Committee; and the Episcopal Public Policy Network. Some of the newer advocacy groups were launched by influential and wealthy individuals concerned about the deepening urgency of Africa's problems. DATA was founded by Bill Gates, Jr, of Microsoft, the financier and philanthropist George Soros, and businessman/philanthropist Edward W. Scott, Jr. Scott is also a force behind Friends of the Global Fight Against AIDS, Tuberculosis, and Malaria, which advocates on behalf of the Geneva-based Global Fund to Fight AIDS, Tuberculosis and Malaria.[20]

Some advocacy organizations, such as Bread for the World and Church World Service, attempt to influence Congress by organizing letter-writing campaigns from constituents. Members of Congress, always thinking about the next election, must pay attention. Advocacy groups also seek meetings with members and congressional staff, sometimes taking with them visitors from Africa to speak of their concerns on an issue. Staff of the Africa subcommittees of the House Committee on International Relations and the Senate Committee on Foreign Relations are particularly important contacts, as are the personal staff of the members of those subcommittees. Contacts on the subcommittees on foreign operations of the House and Senate committees on appropriations are vital for issues related to foreign aid and AIDS spending. In addition, advocacy groups provide or suggest witnesses for congressional hearings on African issues, or for 'briefings' of the Congressional Human Rights Caucus, founded by Representative Tom Lantos of California in 1983. Typical briefings have dealt with food aid to Darfur, the AIDS pandemic, and the situation in northern Uganda.

The forty-three-member Congressional Black Caucus (CBC) has been a key advocacy group for Africa and a vehicle for placing African issues on the congressional agenda. Founded in 1969, the CBC was a major force in the passage of anti-apartheid legislation as well as international AIDS legislation, and it has always stood in support of development and disaster assistance for Africa. Priorities for the Caucus include 'eradicating poverty, hunger and armed conflicts in countries around the world, especially in Africa and the Caribbean,' reducing the burden of debt, and 're-engaging with the United Nations' to promote global health and peace.[21]

Representatives of advocacy organizations, congressional staff, and on occasion members of Congress may interact with executive branch and academic policy experts at meetings or study groups organized by think tanks. The Center for Strategic and International Studies (CSIS) and the Woodrow Wilson International Center for Scholars both have Africa programs that are important sources of new ideas and new thinking about Africa policy. CSIS, the Carnegie Endowment for International Peace, the Council on Foreign Relations, and other organizations regularly produce reports that influence policy. Such organizations are committed to balance and objectivity, but the net effect of their Africa work has been to foster the Africa policy discussion in ways that lead to greater attention and expanded resources for the region. An influential new think tank is the Center for Global Development, founded by Scott and two leading economists in 2001.

More and more in recent years, another base of support for helping Africa has been building in the evangelical Christian movement. Evangelical churches and organizations have expanded their relief and development work in Africa, and their support has helped garner the votes of Republican members of Congress for international AIDS programs and the assistance program known as the 'Child Survival and Health Programs Fund.' The long-term impact of evangelical Christians on Africa policy is not yet clear, and the anti-Muslim views found among some evangelicals could prove problematic, to say the least, should they become influential in Africa policy. But moderate and modernist evangelicals could well become a permanent part of a wider and more effective coalition supporting a fair and just Africa policy – particularly if advocates for Africa in the secular world and in the traditional denominations engage them in dialogue. The concluding chapter will return to this topic.

Other influences on policy

The Heritage Foundation and the American Enterprise Institute (AEI), conservative think tanks, also have Africa programs which host events and issue reports on African issues more in tune with conservative ways of thinking about Africa. Much of their work takes what might be described as a 'business-friendly' approach, arguing in favor of increased market access for US firms in Africa, for example, or efforts to reduce corruption and promote transparency in the region. One might feel that they ought to give more attention to the problems of African access to US markets or to transparency in US public and private dealings with Africa, but their stance represents a positive evolution in conservative thinking about Africa. There was a time not long past, after all, when conservatives wanted close US ties to the Ian Smith regime in Rhodesia, aid to the RENAMO rebels in Mozambique, and support for white minority rule in South Africa.

The Corporate Council on Africa, founded in 1993, has a membership consisting of major and lesser US corporations, and advocates in support of stronger commercial relations between the United States and Africa. It has been a strong backer of the African Growth and Opportunity Act (AGOA) program, discussed in a later chapter. Corporations also employ lobbyists to influence Africa policy, as do some twenty-six African governments.[22] Clearly the influence of corporate lobbyists has been significant on trade and commercial issues, such as intellectual property rights or subsidies for US cotton growers. Some members of Congress and others involved in Africa policy resent being lobbied by professional lobbying firms representing African governments, feeling that this should be the work of African ambassadors and African embassy staff. African governments evidently believe, however, that lobbyists can help them navigate the complex channels of policymaking in Washington. The African diaspora living in the United States also makes its voice heard from time to time, sometimes literally. In May 2006, Ethiopian demonstrators outside the Department of State, protesting the conduct of the Ethiopian parliamentary election and attempting unsuccessfully to persuade US officials to intervene in some way, were audible inside the building.

Conclusion

President George W. Bush came into office in 2000 without any great interest in Africa and certainly with no conviction that the region was important to the United States. His ties to an evangelical Christian base, combined with pressures from Congress and advocates for Africa, pushed him to respond to the situation in southern Sudan and the AIDS crisis, and to increase aid to the region. But the dictates of political realism, which has always devalued Africa as a foreign policy concern for the United States, have continued to restrict US engagement with the region. Meanwhile, the Global War on Terror, inspired by neoconservative thinking, and self-interested concerns over oil imports, threaten to undercut efforts to achieve a fairer and more just Africa policy. GWOT in particular may be pushing the United States into actions that could prove destabilizing for parts of Africa.

2 | Aid, trade, and development: policy improvements less than advertised

Promoting long-term economic development, reducing poverty, and increasing per capita incomes should be the centerpiece of a fair and just Africa policy. The need in Africa is very great. According to the World Bank, poverty rates declined significantly in most of the developing world from 1990 through 2002, but in sub-Saharan Africa the proportion of people living on less than $2 per day remained essentially the same – 75 per cent in 1990 compared with 74.9 per cent in 2002.[1] From 1981 through 2002, the number of Africans living at this level of extreme poverty rose from 288 million to 516 million, and continued increases seemed inevitable.[2] While many sub-Saharan countries are currently experiencing positive GDP growth owing to rising world prices for oil and other natural resources, per capita incomes remain at abysmal levels in most of the region: $270 in 2004 in Mozambique; $380 in Ghana – both often described as 'success stories' due to recent GDP growth; $330 in Mali; and $430 in oil-rich Nigeria.[3] Unless poverty can be reduced and per capita incomes raised, little progress can be made in Africa toward achieving the United Nations Millennium Development Goals (MDGs), which aim at halving extreme poverty and hunger by 2015.[4] As a result, millions in the sub-Saharan region will continue to be denied the opportunity to lead full and productive lives.

The Bush administration maintains that it strongly supports growth and development in Africa. Before leaving for the July 2005 G8 summit at Gleneagles in Scotland, President Bush said that 'We seek progress in Africa and throughout the developing world because conscience demands it.'[5] In September, he affirmed before the UN General Assembly's 2005 World Summit that 'We must defend and extend a vision of human dignity, and opportunity, and prosperity ... To spread a vision of hope, the United States is determined to help nations that are struggling with poverty. We are committed to the Millennium Development Goals.'[6]

The administration argues that it is promoting development in Africa through increased foreign assistance, trade promotion via the African Growth and Opportunity Act (AGOA) program, support for the reduction of trade barriers, and debt relief. US aid to Africa has indeed increased, but by far the largest increases have come through the President's Emergency Plan for AIDS Relief (PEPFAR) and other emergency and humanitarian programs, rather than in programs directly focused on reducing poverty and raising incomes.

The administration's Millennium Challenge Account (MCA) promises a significant additional aid increase for Africa, but the MCA has never been fully funded by Congress and has been slow to make grants to date. Its potential for helping large numbers of Africa's poor is limited by the strict criteria the administration has imposed for grant eligibility. AGOA is also a limited program showing only modest successes, while decisive actions to eliminate US barriers to African trade have yet to be taken. A debt forgiveness package agreed to by the G8 at Gleneagles in 2006 is quite modest; and any gains from debt reduction may be offset by cuts in multilateral development assistance.

The Bush administration has announced various other initiatives for Africa, but these are not well funded. The Initiative to End Hunger in Africa, announced in 2002, has no specified overall funding target and it is not clear that the initiative has generated resources that would not otherwise have gone to agriculture projects under pre-existing programs. The multi-year Africa Education Initiative is to cost just $600 million in total. The five-year initiative for fighting malaria in Africa, begun in

2005, is funded more substantially at $1.2 billion, but defers the bulk of its spending until 2009 and 2010,[7] after President Bush has left office and to a time when the overall US budget situation is likely to be precarious owing to the administration's hefty domestic tax cuts.

If the United States is to make a larger contribution to fighting poverty in Africa, it will have to fund a much more substantial development assistance program with a stronger focus on strengthening infrastructure, higher education, agriculture,[8] and other sectors that make a direct contribution to economic growth. The United States should take the lead in achieving more sweeping debt relief and a real reduction in trade barriers. New and creative ways should be found for promoting US trade with Africa, as well as investments by firms that can create jobs and develop Africa's infrastructure. The Middle East, the Global War on Terror, and other issues are dominating the foreign policy agenda, however, and the US budget is sorely constrained by vast annual deficits. Agricultural lobbies opposed to trade reform remain powerful. Thus, there seems little reason to hope for substantial new commitments to reducing poverty and raising incomes in the near future.

Assistance programs

Bush administration officials often boast that the United States has sharply increased aid to Africa. Indeed, the President said in June 2005, before leaving for Gleneagles, that he had tripled aid over levels seen in the Clinton administration – although in fact the actual increase in aid as normally measured was considerably less than this. Foreign aid data are usually reported in terms of obligations made in a fiscal year, rather than actual disbursements. In the fiscal 2001 budget, which was prepared by the Clinton administration before Bush took office and was little changed by the new administration, the United

TABLE 2.1 US economic and humanitarian aid to sub-Saharan Africa (fiscal years, millions of current dollars)

Program	2002	2003	2004	2005	2006E	2007R
Development assistance	454.0	490.7	466.7	517.5	588.5	563.5
Child survival and health	424.4	541.1	477.3	370.3	391.9	478.5
Global HIV/AIDS initiative	0	0	263.8	885.7	1,238.7	1,994.0
Liberia supplemental	0	0	200.0	0	0	0
Sudan/Africa supplemental	0	90.0	107.9	0	0	0
Economic Support Fund	120.0	109.4	74.1	126.2	121.3	164.3
Peace Corps	53.7	63.3	62.2	75.7	68.7	66.8
Millennium Challenge Compacts	0	0	219.9	307.3	– [a]	– [a]
Millennium Threshold Programs	0		11.2	33.8	– [a]	– [a]
Emergency food aid	462.9	1,165.9	1,187.9	1,234.7	547.7[b]	217.5[a]
African Development Foundation	16.5	18.7	18.6	18.8	22.8	22.7
Migration/refugee assistance	187.5	228.5	226.4	418.2	245.5	235.9
African Development Bank	5.1	5.1	5.1	4.1	3.6	5.0
African Development Fund	100.0	107.4	112.1	105.2	134.3	135.7
Total	1,824.1	2,820.1	3,433.2	4,097.5	3,363.0	3,883.9

Notes: a. Data not yet available. b. These amounts are expected to increase substantially as additional food aid is provided from the emergency food reserve. See text. E = estimate, R = requested.

States committed approximately $1.7 billion in economic aid to Africa. By fiscal 2004, the year the administration uses for calculating its comparison to the Clinton administration and its promise of a future doubling, US obligations had reached only about double the 2001 amount.[9] In claiming a tripling, the Bush administration was using disbursement data for 2000 compiled by the Organization for Economic Cooperation and Development (OECD), which would have included obligations made in earlier budgets, rather than the Clinton administration's peak obligations which took effect in 2001.[10] It was at Gleneagles that Bush promised a further doubling of aid to Africa by 2010 (after he leaves office), as compared to 2004.

Table 2.1, based on data compiled by the Congressional Research Service of the US Library of Congress, shows US economic and humanitarian assistance obligations to sub-Saharan Africa during the fiscal years (which begin in October of the preceding year) in which the Bush administration has had full control over the foreign assistance budget. It includes estimated aid in fiscal 2006 (2006E) and the administration's request for aid in fiscal 2007 (2007R).[11]

The table indicates that US economic and humanitarian assistance to Africa could well double by 2010, compared with 2004, even in terms of obligations. The increase in total obligations from fiscal 2004 to fiscal 2005 was $664 million, and if this pace of growth is maintained through fiscal 2010, an additional $3.98 billion would flow to the region – well above the $3.43 billion required for a doubling. True, the amounts *currently* estimated to go to Africa in 2006 and requested for 2007 are well below the actual 2005 amount, but the 2006 and 2007 totals are certain to increase as the United States allocates additional food aid from its emergency food reserve. If recent years are any indication, this additional aid could reach as much as $1 billion or more, although global food emergencies are straining the reserve.[12] Congress seems committed to meeting Africa's food aid needs, however, and in the Iraq war/Katrina hurricane emergency supplemental appropriation, passed in June 2006, it set aside $350 million in added food aid for Darfur, Chad, and East Africa.[13] Further aid increases for Africa are expected through the Millennium Challenge Account (MCA) program, even though Congress is not funding this program at the levels sought by the administration.

Budget shortfalls in the United States could reduce planned aid increases for sub-Saharan Africa, and Bono has already expressed his concerns over budget decisions in the US Congress that may reduce worldwide foreign assistance funding for fiscal 2007.[14] The impact of these decisions on spending for Africa is not yet known, and it may be that the region will escape largely unscathed. In past years, Congress has added funds to the administration's budget request for development and fighting AIDS worldwide, making more available for Africa than the administration had requested. Whether Congress can continue to do this, in view of the US budget situation, remains to be seen, although the Democratic Party majorities taking over Congress in 2007 are likely to be sympathetic to Africa and its needs. The change in the presidency that will take place in January 2009 could also affect aid to Africa, although in ways that cannot now be foreseen. For the moment, in any event, the administration's target of doubling aid to Africa by 2010 appears in range.

The increase in aid to Africa is surely a significant development in US relations with the region, and has persuaded columnist Nicholas Kristof, a strong critic of Darfur policy, to entitle an essay 'Bush, a friend of Africa.'[15] The administration has not only mobilized more resources for Africa than its predecessor, but it has also pushed the United States well into the lead as a provider to Africa of Official Development Assistance (ODA), a broad measure of aid that promotes economic development and welfare developed by the OECD.[16] In former years, France and sometimes Britain typically gave more. The United States still ranks well behind several donors, however, in terms of the percentage of aid going to Africa – giving 22 per cent of its ODA to the region in 2004, compared with 53 per cent for France, 42 per cent for Britain, and an impressive 71 per cent for Ireland.[17]

The great question for those seeking a better future for Africa is whether the growth in US aid will contribute to long-term poverty reduction and to lasting increases in incomes. Table 2.1 indicates that a significant portion of the increase results from emergency food aid being provided in response to drought and humanitarian crises. Each year, the administration requests and Congress approves a specific amount of food aid for Africa, and then, as noted above, additional food aid has been supplied from the US emergency food reserve as emergencies develop. Responding to African emergencies is a moral responsibility, and a January 2006 report on Africa policy by a Council on Foreign Relations independent task force notes that 'Americans can and should feel proud of their country's contributions.' But the report added that 'the United States must not confuse emergency aid with long term investments for development. Steady increases in the latter cannot be sacrificed to the sporadic demands for emergency aid.'[18]

Unfortunately, the United States provides food aid to Africa in the form of commodities, and this can actually work against economic development by driving down prices paid to African farmers. Development experts have long recognized that it is far better to provide food relief to the poor by giving them money so that they can purchase food on local markets from African producers. But as Peter Timmer of the Center for Global Development points out,

> For 50 years, the farm bloc, large multinational food processors, the US shipping industry, and charitable organizations engaged in relief and development activities in poor countries have

> supported generous funding for America's food aid program. All of the food provided through this program was grown in the US, processed by US firms, shipped on US bottoms [ships], and distributed through US-based agencies and organizations.[19]

To his credit, Andrew Natsios, who directed the US Agency for International Development (USAID) under President Bush from May 2001 to January 2006, supported an initiative to replace some commodity aid with cash. His 2005 attempt to secure $300 million for food aid purchases in Africa was not, however, strongly backed by the administration and went down to defeat in Congress in the face of opposition from the farm lobby, agribusiness, the shipping industry, and the non-governmental organizations (NGOs) that distribute food aid.[20] For fiscal 2007, the administration asked that 25 per cent of food aid funds be used for local and regional procurement of commodities, but Congress was not expected to approve.

By far the greatest increase in US aid to Africa is occurring in the Global HIV/AIDS Initiative, which is channeling large amounts principally to twelve 'focus countries' in the region. Like food aid, this is an emergency program – indeed, it is the principal component of the President's Emergency Plan for AIDS Relief – rather than a program aimed directly at promoting economic development. Of course, PEPFAR, which will be discussed in the next chapter, will contribute to development by strengthening health delivery systems, training African health personnel, keeping parents alive to raise their children, and in other ways. But prevention messages, condoms for 'at risk' populations, antiretroviral treatments, and improvements in care for patients and orphans, however valuable and morally essential, are not going to make the same kind of direct contribution to long-term growth as a railway rehabilitation project, a new agricultural college, or fellowships for graduate students in engineering. The United

States has been largely out of the business of providing this sort of aid for decades owing to concerns over corruption, creating 'white elephant' projects that are not maintained, and other issues. In the 1970s, Congress decided to focus aid on helping the poorest of the poor and meeting basic human needs, while in the late 1980s and through the 1990s, the emphasis shifted to promoting economic policy reforms and strengthening the private sector.[21] Some recognition of the importance of infrastructure is now dawning on policymakers, however, and the Millennium Challenge Account grants typically include infrastructure components. The Ghana grant, for example, includes an upgrade of the highway from the international airport to Accra, the capital. But as noted above, only a few African countries are likely to benefit from the MCA for some time to come.

These shifting emphases in US foreign assistance policy arise from real problems that are present in Africa and affect the region's prospects for development. But in the Bush administration, as in its predecessors, there has been a failure of creative thinking on new ways to deal with these problems and on new ways to generate the resources that would be needed to overcome them. It is easier to step away from building infrastructure than to grapple with the difficult questions of how port facilities, roads, railways, schools, teaching hospitals, and universities can be financed and maintained. It is easier to win public and congressional support for responding to the AIDS pandemic, particularly when church groups and activists are demanding that more be done, than to find the even greater resources that would be needed for Africa's economic recovery.

The other programs listed in Table 2.1 also make only limited contributions toward promoting long-term growth and development. The Child Survival and Health Programs Fund, created by Congress in 1995, supports infectious disease prevention, immunizations, and the President's malaria initiative. Like the PEPFAR program, these efforts are highly worthwhile on humanitarian grounds, and healthy people are far more able to contribute to economic development than the sick. Moreover, by expanding the health sector, health programs are creating jobs and rebuilding health infrastructure. But the impact of health programs would be greatly enhanced if the United States were also doing more to strengthen African economies overall. Poor people benefit from improved health, to be sure, but they still need employment.

The Economic Support Fund (ESF) is an economic assistance program specifically aimed at promoting US political and security interests first and foremost, rather than development, and its use is more and more controlled by the Department of State rather than USAID. ESF aid can be helpful to development – most of the new US aid going to Liberia is ESF aid and will help stabilize the country as it emerges from its long nightmare of civil war. But ESF is being used for Liberia precisely because it is a flexible aid channel that can be quickly programmed. Its primary value to policymakers is for achieving short-term, political outcomes. The Peace Corps, which has had a modest expansion in Africa under President Bush, provides help at the local level to Africa's poor, but aims more at promoting mutual understanding than development. The African Development Foundation is a small-scale program established by Congress in 1980 out of a concern that too little US assistance was reaching the poor at the grass roots in Africa. The Foundation make grants to community-based self-help organizations, and while its work is praiseworthy, its budget has always been limited.

The United States does support long-term development through its contributions to the World Bank's International Development Association (IDA) and to the multilateral African Development Bank Group, which includes the African Development Fund program with a focus on poor countries. But apart from these contributions, the principal US aid programs supporting such development are the Development Assistance (DA) program and the Millennium Challenge Account. DA has certainly not been a priority for the Bush administration in Africa. Indeed, its DA budget request for fiscal 2006 was $428.5 million, less than the $433.6 million it had requested for fiscal 2002. The level of this request was particularly surprising because two of President Bush's much-touted Africa initiatives – the Initiative to End Hunger and the Africa Education Initiative – are funded through DA. Fortunately, as has happened in other years, Congress appropriated more for Development Assistance worldwide than the administration requested in 2006, allowing more to be provided to Africa; but as noted above this practice may prove difficult to continue. The $563 million requested for 2007 was a considerable step forward from the 2006 request – an increase probably made necessary by the President's Gleneagles pledge. It is still $25 million less than the amount made available by Congress for 2006, however, and the $490 requested for fiscal 2008 would represent a significant setback for the program.

Millennium Challenge Account

With the DA program for Africa growing slowly, the Millennium Challenge Account remains the one vehicle through which the Bush administration might achieve a large boost in assistance targeted directly toward economic development. President Bush announced the MCA initiative in a March 2002 appearance with Bono at the Inter-American Development Bank in Washington. The MCA was to phase in a $5 billion increase in annual US assistance worldwide over three years – a goal that has never been reached because of congressional reservations about the program. Congress has consistently appropriated less than requested for the MCA, in part because the program is new and untested, and because of the slow pace at which the Millennium Challenge Corporation (MCC), established to implement the program, has disbursed funds. Moreover, Congress has wanted to use some of the funds freed up by reduced support for the MCA to provide larger amounts than requested for other programs. As a result, just $1.75 billion was appropriated for the MCA in fiscal 2006, when the program should have reached its $5 billion goal. The administration requested $3 billion for fiscal 2007[22] and the same amount for fiscal 2008, but substantially smaller amounts are likely to be available.

The MCA is likely to have a modest impact in Africa as a whole, at least in the near future, not only because its budget remains limited but also because the MCC has established a set of criteria for eligibility that few African countries are able to meet. President Bush said that MCA assistance would go to countries that 'live by these three broad standards – ruling justly, investing in their people, and encouraging economic freedom,'[23] and the MCC measures these by sixteen explicit criteria. One measure of 'ruling justly,' for example, is an index of civil liberties created by Freedom House, a US-based non-governmental organization, while 'economic freedom' is measured in part through a World Bank estimate of the number of days required to start a business.

These criteria can serve a useful purpose to the extent that they inspire governments to undertake needed economic reforms. But most African countries, including populous countries with substantial economic weight, such as Nigeria and Ethiopia, are not likely to be able to meet the criteria for years to come. By 2006, just twelve countries, most of them fairly small in terms of population, had been found eligible: Benin, Burkina Faso, Cape Verde, Gambia, Ghana, Lesotho, Madagascar, Mali, Mozambique, Namibia, Senegal, and Tanzania. It may be a hopeful sign, however, that Kenya and Uganda have been declared 'threshold' countries, eligible for grants to help them improve their performance so that they might meet the MCC criteria in the future. Even after becoming eligible, a country must submit a proposal, prepared with broad civil society participation, before it can enter into a 'compact' with the MCC and begin to receive assistance. Only three African countries, Madagascar, Cape Verde, and Benin, had completed this process by 1 August 2006, when Ghana signed an accord as well. MCC amounts flowing to Africa may be expected to continue to increase as Senegal and other countries come into the program, but most of Africa's poor will not see any benefit from the MCA soon. It is worrisome, moreover, that the administration's request for USAID Development Assistance in Benin and Madagascar in fiscal 2007 is below the level expected to be provided in 2006. This raises the possibility that policymakers are viewing MCA aid to some extent as a replacement for ordinary development aid, rather than as additional assistance.

Transformational development?

Planning documents and other publications of the MCA and USAID under the Bush administration are suffused with the language of 'transformational development,' which aims at promoting 'far reaching, fundamental changes in governance and institutions, human capacity, and economic structure, so that countries can sustain further economic and social progress without depending on foreign aid.'[24] 'Transformational development' has a certain evangelical ring to it, but the term basically reflects the administration's neoliberal, free market economic orientation, combined with advocacy of good governance, transparency, and fiscal responsibility as urged by development experts for years. There is a certain irony in US championship of responsible economic policy, in view of America's own huge budget and trade deficits, although no one denies that African economic development would benefit from genuine economic reforms. Whether aid agencies know how to use foreign aid to promote such reforms, however, or have succeeded in doing so, is far from clear. According to the USAID budget justification for

2006, there have been important gains: 'Africa's prospects for a better future continue to brighten as many countries in the region are beginning to reap the benefits of economic policy changes, improved governance and investments in key social sectors undertaken during the past decade.'[25] Perhaps it will one day be shown that the positive GDP growth currently taking place in several African countries is attributable to economic reforms pushed by Western donors, but the increase in the price of oil and other resources seems as likely an explanation. Meanwhile, many are concerned that African governments have been able to minimize the impact of reforms on traditional ways of doing business, including widespread corruption characterized by political scientists as 'clientelism' or 'neopatrimonialism.' The resulting partial reforms have been accompanied in many instances by a decline in the capacity of African governments to deliver social services,[26] and this seems to be true of several leading African recipients of US assistance, such as Kenya, Uganda, and Nigeria.

Nonetheless, the themes of 'transformational development' continue to be reflected in actual US assistance programs. Development funds are being spent for 'strengthening market-oriented economic analysis' in Angola, boosting 'knowledge management' in Ethiopia, or promoting 'increased competitiveness' in Zambia.[27] This sort of aid, while it may have some as yet unproven value , will not be sufficient to put Africa on the path to development. The Council on Foreign Relations independent task force on Africa policy argued that the United States has 'unrealized potential' to help Africa in a number of other areas no longer being emphasized, including agricultural development, basic education, higher education, and science and technology. (The task force also pointed out that population programs have been unwisely de-emphasized in the US assistance program owing in part to 'religious and political opposition to some family planning programs.')[28] Former World Bank official William Easterly has taken a different approach and called for refocusing aid on helping the poor – providing such aid even in countries that are not democratic or well governed:

> Put the focus back where it belongs: get the poorest people in the world such obvious goods as the vaccines, the antibiotics, the food supplements, the improved seeds, the fertilizer, the roads, the boreholes, the textbooks, and the nurses. That is not making the poor dependent on handouts: it is giving the poorest people the health, nutrition, education, and other inputs that raise the payoff to their own efforts to better their lives.[29]

Easterly and the Council task force are arguing powerfully, if in different ways, for major changes in assistance policy.

The changes sought by Easterly are the more sweeping because he wants a comprehensive restructuring of the Western development aid system in ways that would empower the poor, in Africa and elsewhere, to obtain assistance that would directly meet their needs. He is highly skeptical, to say the least, of economist Jeffrey Sachs's contention, which was influential on the Gleneagles summit, that large aid increases are needed to promote a 'big push' in public investments.[30] Easterly's ideas are intriguing, but at the same time it seems to this author that Africa also wants and needs major improvements in infrastructure in order to expand economic opportunity for the poor, just as it needs help with peacekeeping and conflict recovery to establish a growth-friendly environment. Progress in these areas would be truly transforming, but infrastructure, peacekeeping, and recovery are expensive and will require large aid increases, just as Sachs has proposed. Ongoing study, evaluation, and re-examination are also needed as aid increases go forward in order to combat waste and assure that aid is used as effectively as possible. Perhaps such studies would conclude that a combination of approaches to development, including those advocated by Easterly, is warranted.

The point here, however, is that the Bush administration appears not to be engaged in ongoing study and re-examination of the best ways to promote development, but instead seems to have brought innovation to a halt with the creation of the MCC. Congress has launched a study of 'what works' in foreign assistance programs, to be prepared by the Commission on Helping to Enhance the Livelihood of People Around the Globe (HELP Commission), but this report will not be completed until 2008, as the Bush administration leaves office. The Commission aspires to issue a document that will 'avoid the fate of most such commission reports that end up occupying space on a bookshelf and making little difference in policy.'[31] Whether it succeeds in this remains to be seen.

Meanwhile, the administration is proceeding with a reform of foreign assistance programs that will likely bring political concerns rather than development objectives increasingly to the fore. Secretary of State Condoleezza Rice announced on 16 January 2006 that as part of the administration's commitment to 'transformational diplomacy' – that evangelical term again – a new post was being created: Director of Foreign Assistance. The Director, Randall Tobias, a former pharmaceutical company executive, has little development background, apart from serving as the first head of the State Department's Global HIV/AIDS Initiative, which coordinates PEPFAR. His office as Director, like the PEPFAR office, is at the Department of State and reports directly to Rice. Tobias serves concurrently as Administrator of the US Agency for International Development. This arrangement seems certain to assure that USAID programs will more and more reflect the foreign policy agenda of the administration, rather than a long-term development agenda. Nor is it certain that the reorganization will achieve greater coherence in aid programs, as the administration desires. The coordinator provides only 'guidance' to the MCC, for example, and the extent to which he will be able to influence its work is not yet clear. It would have been far better, as foreign assistance experts Carol Lancaster and Ann Van Dusen have argued, to centralize US foreign assistance programs in a single department of development, as Britain has done. In that way, a distinct and coordinated development agenda would be represented at the cabinet level by a Secretary of International Development.[32]

Trade and investment policy

President Bush has said that 'open trade and international investment are the surest and fastest ways for Africa to make progress,'[33] and in speeches, documents, and reports his officials have repeatedly asserted that an expansion of US–Africa trade and investment ties is central to US development policy for the region. Hardworking staff at USAID, the Office of the United States Trade Representative, and elsewhere in government have devoted considerable time and energy to these efforts, but real progress is difficult to discern. US trade with sub-Saharan Africa has grown owing to rising imports of African oil, but was only about 1.9 per cent of America's trade with the world as a whole in 2004, the last year for which comparative data are available – hardly a major improvement over the 1.5 per cent level seen in 2001.[34] The dollar value of US investment in Africa has also grown somewhat, but was just 0.7 per cent of US foreign investment worldwide in 2005.[35] US investors, concerned about political risk, lack of transparency, and crime, continue to regard the sub-Saharan region as marginal at best. To counter these problems, the Council on Foreign Relations task force has urged policymakers to consider tax incentives, such as a zero tax on repatriated profits, to persuade US firms to invest in Africa, as well as partnerships between US government agencies and private companies for infrastructure projects.[36] China is forging ahead with such partnerships around the continent, but Africa probably ranks too low on the Bush administration policy agenda to merit the effort and imagination required to launch a comparable American effort.

AGOA The African Growth and Opportunity Act (AGOA) program was created by Congress in 2000,[37] with the support of the Clinton administration, as a way of expanding Africa's access to US markets. It is constantly cited by policymakers as evidence that the United States is facilitating Africa's entry into the global economy. AGOA has indeed been beneficial, and AGOA officials cite a number of successes, as mentioned below. But the program's overall impact has been quite limited, and more will have to be done if Africa's trade is to be given a real boost by the United States.

AGOA offers duty-free access to the United States for a wide range of African products. There are a number of conditions for participation in the program – participants should have market-based economies, be fighting corruption, eliminate barriers to US trade and investment, and respect intellectual property rights, among other requirements – but these have not been rigorously interpreted and some thirty-seven countries have been declared eligible to participate. Textile interests in the United States succeeded in attaching a requirement that yarn and fabric used in assembling apparel for export to the United States be sourced in Africa itself or from the United States, but friends of Africa in Congress managed to add a Lesser Developed Country (LDC) exception that temporarily allows twenty-two African countries to obtain these inputs anywhere. AGOA had initially been set to expire in 2008, and the LDC exception in 2004, but Congress has granted an extension to 2015 for the overall program and until September 2007 for the LDC exception.[38] The rationale behind the shorter LDC extension was that a deadline would encourage African countries to develop their own fabric-production industries, although skeptics argued that the time allowed was too short. This issue has been rendered largely moot by the recent sharp decline in African apparel exports to the United States, discussed below. USAID and other agencies have launched programs to help African countries build trade capacity so that they can participate in the program, and the United States has established 'Regional Hubs for Global Competitiveness' for East and Central Africa, Southern Africa, and West Africa.

Successes claimed by AGOA include growing exports to the United States of frozen fruit sorbets from South Africa, bird-seed from Ethiopia, woodcarvings and handicrafts from West Africa, and various apparel items from around the region.[39] While these gains have been important for the companies and workers involved, the overall statistics are not encouraging. True, AGOA reports an overall 44 per cent increase in imports from AGOA participating countries in 2005, but this increase results from soaring US oil imports, which grew by 53 per cent. Non-oil AGOA exports actually fell by 16 per cent because of a decline in US imports of apparel from Africa.[40] This decline results from the January 2005 expiration of the international Multi-Fiber Agreement which had permitted restrictions on imports of apparel to the United States and other developed countries from low-cost producers, particularly China and India, through a system of quotas. The African textile sector is now paying the price, even though the US and other governments have imposed limits on the rate at which Chinese apparel imports can grow. Meanwhile, the African textile sector is suffering increased competition from China and India for domestic markets in Africa. Conceivably, a few AGOA countries will benefit from the rise in revenues resulting from their oil exports to the United States, but as a later chapter, dealing with US policy on democracy, will note, oil revenues have special problems that undercut their potential contribution to poverty reduction.

The Office of the United States Trade Representative issued a report in July 2005 that identified reasons for the failure of AGOA to make a larger contribution to African growth. Many of these had to do with the unfavorable policy environments in African countries, lack of transparency, and other governance problems that the United States and the international financial institutions have focused on for years with minimal success. But the report highlighted other problems as well, including 'inadequate transportation infrastructure, such as a lack of good road and railway networks, or seaport and airport services'; and 'inadequate telecommunications and expensive and/or unreliable utilities such as water and electricity ...'[41] In other words, Africa needs costly infrastructure development – and by implication more development assistance focused on infrastructure – if it is to benefit fully from AGOA. As argued above, prospects for increased US aid of this sort are not bright.

Trade barriers President Bush and officials of his administration insist that free markets are a key component of any solution to Africa's development problems, but in fact the United States does not practise free market principles when it comes to international trade in agricultural commodities. The European Union has perhaps been a greater offender in this area over the years, but subsidies paid by the US government to American farmers create a global oversupply of commodities produced in Africa and reduce prices paid to African farmers. The OECD estimates total US official support to agriculture – including support to producers of maize, rice, sorghum, sugar, peanuts (groundnuts), and other crops produced in Africa – at $108.7 billion,[42] an amount that far exceeds the GDP of any sub-Saharan country with the exception of South Africa.

Cotton subsidies, usually estimated at about $3 billion per year, have come in for particular criticism because they weaken the ability of West and Central Africa cotton growers to compete in world markets. Oxfam estimated the losses to cotton farmers in these regions at $305 million in 2001 alone.[43] Because of a World Trade Organization decision resulting from a complaint by Brazil, the United States has been forced to end a program that subsidized US cloth manufacturers for using more expensive US-produced cotton. Cotton growers may, however, receive additional payments from other programs to make up for any loss suffered – and other subsidies continue.[44]

The Bush administration's response to criticisms of trade barriers that harm African producers is to insist that it is all in favor of removing those that are unfair and trade-distorting. The near-complete lack of progress in doing so, however, has undermined American credibility on the issue. Neither the President nor Congress seem likely to seriously engage the powerful farm lobbies on subsidies, despite whatever promises US officials may make.

President Bush did remark at the September 2005 UN World Summit that 'the Secretary General said that we ... need to reduce trade barriers and subsidies that are holding developing countries back. I agree with the Secretary General.' On 30 June 2005, before leaving for the Gleneagles G8 meeting, he spoke warmly in support of the Doha Round of trade negotiations, named for the city in Qatar where the negotiations were launched in 2001:

> Now we must take the next large step: expanding the entire global trading system through the Doha negotiations. The World Bank estimates that completing these negotiations could add $350 billion annually to developing countries' incomes, and lift 140 million people out of poverty. The Doha negotiations are the most practical and important anti-poverty initiative in the world, and we must bring them to a prompt and successful conclusion.[45]

Yet the Doha Round seems hopelessly stalled on a host of issues – including US insistence that it will act decisively on domestic subsidies only when Europe reduces its tariffs, as well as US demands that developing countries open their markets to US agricultural products. US complaints about the intransigence of the other parties to the Doha process have become a convenient excuse for doing nothing with respect to American subsidies. The European Union maintains that it is willing to make new concessions to the developing world on agricultural trade and has called on the United States to come forward with new proposals. At a September 2006 meeting held to discuss the issue, US Trade Representative Susan Schwab defended the administration's refusal to do so by saying that in the United States 'being a champion of small family farms cuts across party lines'[46] – as if the world were unaware of the role played by agribusiness in forming US policy on subsidies. The President's 'fast track authority,' which would limit congressional debate over any agreement reached – and make adoption more likely – expires in July 2007. Congress may balk at renewing it, and the Doha window of opportunity for a subsidy reduction pact could well disappear.

Friends of Africa would welcome some creative, 'outside the box' thinking on trade barriers from the administration, perhaps leading to the unilateral removal or substantial reduction of the most harmful or to a compensation program for African producers that are damaged by them. On current evidence, there is little reason to expect this to occur.

New thinking is also needed from US officials on the negotiations, which began in 2003 with South Africa and the four other members of the Southern African Customs Union (SACU), on a free trade agreement (FTA). An FTA could be risky for the region if it opens SACU to unfettered competition from US business and agricultural conglomerates; but at the same time, it could help by locking in the AGOA tariff concessions beyond 2015 and by bringing in new, employment-generating investment.

The negotiations are held behind closed doors and any draft

agreement is secret, but the information that seeps out indicates that the administration is pursuing a sweeping accord fully in keeping with its avowed neoliberal, free market ideology. Reports suggest, for example, that the United States wants unfettered rights for US companies to export to southern Africa, to compete for government contracts, and to provide essential services, such as supplying water and electricity.[47] Stiff intellectual property requirements that could affect the price of medicines are evidently being sought as well. US competition with infant industries and local farmers, or participation by private US companies in critical services, are inevitably sensitive issues, as Americans should understand. There was a furor in the United States itself in early 2004 over the planned takeover of the management of several ports by a Dubai-based company, as well as a major controversy in 2005 over the attempt by the China National Offshore Oil Corporation to purchase UNOCAL, a US petroleum firm. The Dubai ports deal was postponed as a result of the protests and remains in limbo, while CNOOC eventually withdrew its offer for UNOCAL shares. South African negotiators are also concerned that unregulated competition from US firms in investment and government contracts could undermine the Black Economic Empowerment program, intended to right some of the wrongs of apartheid. Surely some concessions could be made to the emerging SACU economies on special protections for critical services and industries, and for farmers; as well as on intellectual property rights and other issues. But concessions do not seem likely, and with the President's fast track authority expiring, the US–SACU talks on an FTA may well fail.

Debt

At the 2005 Gleneagles summit, the G8 agreed to complete forgiveness of debt to the multilateral development banks and the International Monetary Fund for eighteen poor countries, including fourteen in Africa, that have completed the World Bank/IMF Heavily Indebted Poor Countries (HIPC) initiative process. In addition, the G8 endorsed an innovative debt relief program for Nigeria, including $18 billion in debt forgiveness and a Nigerian payment of $12 billion. These are real achievements, and represent a considerable victory for the Jubilee 'drop the debt' campaign, with strong roots in the faith community and among the broader coalition of development advocates. Todd Moss of the Center for Global Development in Washington has argued that campaigners may have exaggerated the impact debt forgiveness will have on economic growth or the ability of poor countries to provide social services.[48] At the same time, Moss points out that at least the moral absurdity of impoverished countries being required to make payments to the rich has been eased.

The impact of debt forgiveness in Africa will likely be limited because of the small number of countries that are eligible. There are nineteen other poor African countries that are enrolled in HIPC but not yet at the completion point – and hence ineligible for debt forgiveness for the present. Countries outside HIPC also have serious debts but are ineligible for debt forgiveness altogether. Perhaps the saddest case is Kenya, with a $7 billion debt and a vast population of very poor people, but regarded by donors as capable of repaying because exports supposedly make its debt burden 'sustainable.' More needs to be done to help Kenya and the other countries in Africa whose debt continues to hamper the efforts to realize the Millennium Development Goals.

The Bush administration has supported debt forgiveness but under a peculiar formula that may largely nullify any beneficial effect. The British had proposed before Gleneagles that the developed countries simply assume Africa's debt payments to the World Bank's International Development Association (IDA), the principal creditor; but the Bush administration wanted this debt covered by the Bank itself, which would reduce its loans to poor countries by an amount equal to the debt being written off.[49] This would have eliminated any budgetary impact for the United States and placed the actual burden of debt forgiveness on the poor countries themselves. The US position prevailed in large part, although it was agreed that IDA resources would be increased somewhat overall. Any increased IDA lending, however, is to be spread around all the eligible countries and is not to be targeted toward those receiving debt relief.[50]

Conclusion

The Bush administration plays up its assistance to sub-Saharan Africa, and there is no denying that aid has increased substantially. The sharp boost in funding for fighting the AIDS pandemic is helping the African poor, as is the continuing US commitment to humanitarian food assistance – although as noted above, providing cash for food purchases in Africa rather than US-grown commodities would show a truer generosity. In the area of trade and investment, US programs are much overrated, and the administration's approach to debt forgiveness takes with one hand what it gives away with the other. If the Bush administration were to try to live up to its rhetorical commitment to African development, it would have to shift its assistance program more toward infrastructure, higher education, agriculture, and other productive sectors that contribute to long-term economic development. This shift would be expensive – and hence it is unlikely. Instead, the entire foreign assistance program is being reorganized to bring it more firmly under the control of the Department of State, which pursues a foreign policy agenda rather than a development agenda. This does not bode well for future US contributions to reducing poverty and raising incomes in Africa.

3 | AIDS policy: substantial new program weakened by unilateralism and controversy

President Bush, as seen in the Introduction, came into office with a disinclination to engage with Africa, but the AIDS pandemic sweeping the continent demanded attention. The scale of the disaster, combined with rising media coverage as well as pressure for action from Congress, activist organizations, faith-based advocates, and others, required a response. In finally launching the five-year, $15 billion President's Emergency Plan for AIDS Relief (PEPFAR) in 2003, President Bush took an important step toward a fairer and more just Africa policy. Sizeable new US resources were mobilized to fight the pandemic, contributing substantially to the expansion of treatment, care, and prevention programs around the continent.

Unfortunately, however, the administration's AIDS program was marred by excessive unilateralism, which undercut the efforts of the new and innovative Global Fund to Fight AIDS, Tuberculosis, and Malaria (GFATM) to increase international resources for fighting AIDS. Moreover, administration concessions to the Christian right in highlighting abstinence-until-marriage programs, limiting condom distribution programs, and discouraging prevention services for prostitutes brought unnecessary controversy to PEPFAR. To some extent, as will be seen, the criticisms of the administration on the abstinence issue were overdone; but the administration was reticent and ineffective in explaining its actual abstinence policy, perhaps since doing so might have provoked criticism in its evangelical base. The net effect of the criticisms and controversies was a palpable loss of momentum in support for PEPFAR that could affect the program's funding prospects when it comes up for renewal in Congress, possibly in 2007. If PEPFAR is to continue beyond 2008, it must be reauthorized before October of that year.

Pressure builds

In December 2000, as the Bush administration was preparing to take office, UNAIDS, the Joint United Nations Program on HIV and AIDS, reported that AIDS had already claimed 17 million African lives. More than 25 million Africans were infected with HIV, and 3.8 million new infections had occurred during the year.[1] In sixteen countries, according to UNAIDS, at least one-tenth of the adult population, aged fifteen to forty-five, was HIV positive; and shocking adult infection rates had been recorded in several southern African countries, including 35.8 per cent in Botswana and 19.9 per cent in South Africa.[2]

Activist organizations that had long urged an expanded US response to the African pandemic, such as ACT UP (AIDS Coalition to Unleash Power) and the Global AIDS Alliance, were continuing to apply pressure as a broader coalition of advocates joined the struggle. Nonetheless, how and whether the administration would expand US AIDS efforts remained highly uncertain. USAID administrator Andrew Natsios caused particular dismay when in June 2001 he told a congressional committee that it would be a mistake for the United States to move into AIDS treatment because Africans would not be able to take medications on a regular basis. 'Many people in Africa have never seen a clock or a watch their entire lives,' he said. 'And if you say, one o'clock in the afternoon, they do not know what you are talking about.'[3] This statement brought cries of outrage, charges of racism, and demands for Natsios' resignation. These were ignored, but the episode seemed to indicate that the administration was not going to finance treatment for Africans with AIDS, even as treatment was becoming increasingly effective and its price was declining. Without treatment, the ill were condemned to death.

Understandably, then, the supporters of a new US AIDS initiative, and one that would include treatment, refused to relent. Economist Jeffrey Sachs, then heading a World Health Organization (WHO) Commission on Macroeconomics and Health, was urging a major commitment of resources, and he met with then National Security Advisor Condoleezza Rice in early 2001 to discuss the issue.[4] Bono played an essential role not only as an advocate but also as a catalyst capable of bringing new and unexpected individuals to the cause. He forged a friendship with then Senator Jesse Helms of North Carolina, helping to convert the conservative Republican into a strong advocate of increased spending on preventing mother-to-child transmission of the HIV virus. 'I'm so ashamed I've done so little' about AIDS in Africa, Helms told a Christian conference meeting in Washington in February 2002.[5] Bono also met with Rice, and in May 2002 famously accompanied then Secretary of the Treasury Paul O'Neill on a ten-day trip around Africa that turned the Secretary into a supporter both of an AIDS initiative and of steps to bring clean water to Africa's poor. O'Neill's independent thinking on these and other issues won him no friends at the White House, unfortunately, and he was dismissed at the end of the year.[6] Church members and leaders, including some evangelicals, were also increasingly influential – Franklin Graham of Samaritan's Purse played a role in converting Senator Helms to international AIDS advocacy, for example.[7] Bono himself cited scripture in meetings with both Helms and Bush to win their support.[8]

Meanwhile, Congress, in responding to the rising tide of public pressure, was considering legislation that would, if passed, have forced the administration to act. In particular, the Senate was considering S. 2525, the United States Leadership Against HIV/AIDS, Tuberculosis, and Malaria Act of 2002, sponsored by Democrat

John Kerry and Republican Bill Frist. This bill was approved by the Senate Foreign Relations Committee on 3 July 2002,[9] and would have required the President to 'establish a comprehensive, integrated, five-year strategy to combat global HIV/AIDS.' S. 2525 authorized $1 billion for the newly created GFATM in fiscal 2003 and $1.2 billion in fiscal 2004. Bilateral AIDS programs would have been funded at $800 million in 2003 and $900 million in 2004. Earlier, the House of Representatives had passed an international AIDS bill, H.R. 2069, with lower spending provisions; and when the Senate acted on the House bill on 12 July 2002, it substituted the provisions and amounts of its own S. 2525. For reasons that were never satisfactorily explained, however, the two differing versions of H.R. 2069 were never brought to a conference between the two houses of Congress to resolve differences, as would normally have been the case. Observers speculate that this was because the Bush administration was already well aware of Senator Kerry's plans to run for the presidency in 2004 and discouraged any congressional action that might put a feather in his cap. Meanwhile, as will be seen below, the administration was concluding that whatever was to be done about the AIDS crisis by the United States should be primarily a bilateral US effort, not one headed by the Global Fund, which would have received more resources than bilateral programs under both versions of H.R. 2069.

PEPFAR is launched

In confidential meetings and discussions in subsequent months, the administration was planning just what the US response would be. According to reports, a critical role was played by a speechwriter and trusted presidential aide, Michael Gerson, an evangelical Christian. Gerson is said to have persuaded Josh Bolten, then the White House Deputy Chief of Staff for Policy, to develop a proposal for a five-year, $15 billion AIDS initiative;

and to have told President Bush, when the proposal was being discussed at a White House meeting, that 'history will judge us severely if we don't do this.'[10] The President's own evangelical leanings may have made him receptive to this appeal. In July 2003, six months after announcing his AIDS initiative – and while on his first and so far only trip to Africa – Bush told The AIDS Support Organization (TASO) in Uganda that 'You know, I believe God has called us into action. I believe we have a responsibility – my country has got a responsibility. We are a great nation, we're a wealthy nation. We have a responsibility to help a neighbor in need, a brother and sister in crisis.'[11]

President Bush hatched his AIDS surprise on 28 January 2003, when, in his annual State of the Union Address, he told a nation he was leading into a war in Iraq that he was also launching an emergency AIDS program. The Iraq war, which began in March, may even have been a factor in the decision to undertake a major AIDS initiative. Many saw the decision as partly designed to show that US foreign policy had a compassionate side and consisted of more than the use of force in pursuit of national interests.[12]

In his address, Bush told the assembled members of Congress and top government officials that

> Today, on the continent of Africa, nearly 30 million people have the AIDS virus – including 3 million children under the age 15. There are whole countries in Africa where more than one-third of the adult population carries the infection. More than 4 million require immediate drug treatment. Yet across that continent, only 50,000 AIDS victims – only 50,000 – are receiving the medicine they need ...
>
> AIDS can be prevented. Anti-retroviral drugs can extend life for many years. And the cost of those drugs has dropped from $12,000 a year to under $300 a year – which places a tremendous possibility within our grasp. Ladies and gentlemen, seldom has

history offered a greater opportunity to do so much for so many.

We have confronted, and will continue to confront, HIV/AIDS in our own country. And to meet a severe and urgent crisis abroad, tonight I propose the Emergency Plan for AIDS Relief – a work of mercy beyond all current international efforts to help the people of Africa. This comprehensive plan will prevent 7 million new AIDS infections, treat at least 2 million people with life-extending drugs, and provide humane care for millions of people suffering from AIDS, and for children orphaned by AIDS.

I ask the Congress to commit $15 billion over the next five years, including nearly $10 billion in new money, to turn the tide against AIDS in the most afflicted nations of Africa and the Caribbean.

The announcement was typical of what has been called the administration's 'appetite for big, visionary ideas, imposed from the top down; an eagerness to centralize decision making in the executive branch; and a tendency to shrug off the advice of experts ...'[13] In the case of PEPFAR, it appears that experts were consulted, but 'surreptitiously'[14] and without a full understanding of what was afoot. A key internal expert, Dr Anthony Fauci, head of the National Institute of Allergy and Infectious Diseases at the National Institutes of Health, was involved from the beginning.[15]

PEPFAR's promise of $15 billion in total spending consisted of $9 billion for fiscal years 2004 through 2008 for fighting AIDS in fourteen (later expanded to fifteen) of the most heavily afflicted countries, including twelve in sub-Saharan Africa: Botswana, Côte d'Ivoire, Ethiopia, Kenya, Mozambique, Namibia, Nigeria, Rwanda, South Africa, Tanzania, Uganda, and Zambia. PEPFAR also promised a total of $1 billion over five years as a US contribution to the Global Fund (see following section), and this amount, together with the $9 billion for the focus countries, constituted the 'new money.' In addition, existing bilateral AIDS programs, principally those of USAID and the Centers for Disease Control and Prevention (CDC) of the Department of Health and Human Services, were incorporated into PEPFAR. These programs were costing about $1 billion per year, and would total $5 billion over five years.

The new funding for the focus countries has been channeled through the Global HIV/AIDS Initiative (GHAI) under the direction of the Office of the Global AIDS Coordinator at the Department of State, a position held by Randall Tobias until he became Director of Foreign Assistance in early 2006. His successor is Mark Dybul, a physician from the US National Institutes of Health, who had helped plan PEPFAR and served as Tobias's deputy. The Coordinator is also responsible for leading the overall US response to the international AIDS crisis and for coordination among the agencies involved.

While PEPFAR has been surrounded by some contentious issues, it is important to pause here and acknowledge that this program represents a major and unprecedented US investment in combating an African health catastrophe. The United States is doing far more for sub-Saharan Africa through PEPFAR than it has done through any other program in the past. US AIDS spending in the region totaled just $441 million in fiscal 2003, but had risen to an estimated $1.4 billion in 2006, with $2.1 billion requested for 2007 and $3.4 billion for 2008.[16] At the outset, there was concern that the administration was requesting less than $3 billion per year for PEPFAR programs worldwide, since that amount seemed to be required to reach a cumulative, five-year total of $15 billion. Officials always insisted, however, that the program needed to 'ramp up' gradually, and by fiscal 2006 PEPFAR spending was exceeding $3 billion. The expectation now is that the $15 billion, five-year total will be reached or even exceeded. A portion of bilateral PEPFAR funds, as well a portion of the US contribution to the Global Fund, goes toward fighting tuberculosis and malaria.

In the early days of the program, critics alleged that PEPFAR funds for AIDS treatment were being wasted because they were being spent on the purchase of high-priced patented medications manufactured by US pharmaceutical companies rather than on inexpensive generic formulations from India, South Africa, and elsewhere. Richard Holbrooke, ambassador to the United Nations in the Clinton administration and head of the Global Business Commission on HIV/AIDS, said in March 2004 that the US delay in purchasing generics was 'tearing apart' the effort to combat AIDS.[17] Claims by US officials that they had to be assured of the quality and safety of generics before using them in a US government program were greeted with skepticism – particularly since they were refusing to use generics already approved by the World Health Organization. Finally, in May 2004, the US Food and Drug Administration instituted an expedited review process for generic formulations. By June 2006, more than twenty generic versions of AIDS drugs by various manufacturers had been approved.

The increase in AIDS spending for Africa through the GHAI program is almost entirely devoted to the twelve focus countries. The criteria for determining which countries are focus countries have never been fully clear, and many in Congress and elsewhere are disturbed that others – such as Malawi, with a 2003 adult infection rate of 14.2 per cent, or Lesotho, with a rate of 28.9 per cent[18] – were not included. Officials point out that such countries can receive grants from the Global Fund, and that they are given AIDS assistance through USAID. This is true even of heavily stricken Zimbabwe, which is otherwise estranged from the United States. Nonetheless, it is unfortunate that PEPFAR was not given a broader sweep.

Global Fund: victim of unilateralism

One of the great disappointments of PEPFAR is its essentially unilateral character and its neglect of the Global Fund to Fight AIDS, Tuberculosis, and Malaria. GFATM devotes about 60 per cent of its resources to fighting AIDS, and channels about 55 per cent to sub-Saharan Africa. US neglect of the Global Fund is a particular tragedy because the Fund was intended to be the principal vehicle for mobilizing additional global resources from other donor countries, foundations, and the private sector for fighting AIDS, tuberculosis, and malaria. It is the principal international funding resource for fighting these diseases in countries that are not PEPFAR focus countries, and the Fund is active even in the focus countries, where US officials acknowledge that its work complements the efforts of PEPFAR. If Global Fund resources are not sharply expanded, the struggle against AIDS worldwide could stagnate; and, since the programs are complementary, the United States might even fail to meet the 2 million treatment objective and other PEPFAR goals set by President Bush. Stephen Lewis, as UN Special Envoy for HIV/AIDS in Africa, was right to observe that the Global Fund is 'the most formidable new international financial mechanism in the battle against communicable disease' and 'deserves every ounce of support it can muster.'[19]

The Global Fund was founded as a wholly new type of organization in the foreign assistance field, with great potential for building local capabilities and assuring accountability. The Fund is not an implementing agency, but rather a 'financial instrument' designed to mobilize, manage, and disburse resources. It operates with a small staff of about two hundred in Geneva, and issues grants in response to applications coming from Country Coordinating Mechanisms (CCMs) in AIDS-afflicted countries.[20] The CCMs in the recipient countries bring together the interested parties or 'stakeholders' to agree on national priorities and to develop and submit coordinated applications to the Fund. CCMs include representatives of government, NGOs, the private sector, multilateral and bilateral aid agencies operating in the country, academic institutions, and people living with the diseases. The applications identify one or more Principal Recipients, such as the national health ministry or one or more NGOs, which are legally responsible for grant implementation. Applications are reviewed by a Technical Review Panel of independent experts, and if a grant is made, the Fund contracts a Local Fund Agent, typically a large accounting firm, to oversee its implementation.

This is just the sort of development model the United States ought to be encouraging – one that supports programs developed in the field by stakeholders working together on a national basis, rather than competing with one another to win resources from a panoply of donors. It strengthens indigenous capabilities by fostering effective planning and building experiences in consultation between government and civil society. The strengths of the approach were recognized by the Bush administration itself, when it created a somewhat similar system for grant awards through the Millennium Challenge Account.

The administration's neglect of the Global Fund seems particularly strange because President Bush himself helped launch the entire project when he made the 'founding pledge' of $200 million in a May 2001 White House Rose Garden ceremony attended by UN Secretary-General Kofi Annan and Nigeria's President Olusegun Obasanjo.[21] US negotiators participated actively in the Transitional Working Group that set up the Fund, helping to establish it as an independent organization with strong mechanisms for monitoring and evaluation.[22] Some trace the subsequent estrangement between the United States and the Global Fund to April 2002, when the Fund's board chose Dr Richard Feachem, a Briton, as Executive Director, rather than an American candidate proposed by the United States.[23] The diplomatic difficulties and criticisms encountered by the United States at the United Nations in the lead-up to the 2003 war in Iraq reinforced sentiments in the administration that were unfriendly toward multilateral organizations generally, and this may also have affected attitudes toward the Global Fund.[24]

In any event, the estrangement was conspicuous, and at a September 2004 closed-door briefing for congressional staff, administration officials launched an unexpected attack on the Global Fund and its management.[25] The officials claimed, among other charges, that the Global Fund was slow to disburse its resources, had insufficient staff, and had disbursed a large initial sum to Ethiopia despite a stated policy of linking disbursements to performance. The Fund moved quickly to try to heal the breach. Feachem drafted a ten-page response for congressional staff, and the Fund's Chief of Operations, Brad Herbert, flew to Washington within days for a round of meetings and briefings.[26] The Fund pointed out that its process at headquarters for making and disbursing grants was moving smoothly, that staff had been added, and that it had been necessary to put a large amount into Ethiopia's account so that the government would have credibility in seeking bids for the purchase of medicines. The Fund also noted that it had dealt expeditiously with problems in recipient countries as they had arisen.

Subsequently, relations between Washington and the Fund seemed to improve, and officials of the Global Fund and PEPFAR went out of their way to exchange complimentary remarks about one another's programs. Their sincerity was difficult to judge, however. Global Fund representatives can hardly afford to offend the United States, which is still the Fund's largest donor, even if it is not giving nearly as much as it should. US officials, who are criticized so often for their go-it-alone approach to foreign affairs, may find it expedient to appear friendly to the Fund.

Contributing far less than needed

US officials are quick to deny short-changing the Global Fund, maintaining that PEPFAR and the Fund are partners cooperating at the headquarters level and in the field. Tobias told a September 2005 pledging conference in London that the US contribution to the Global Fund is a 'strategic priority' for the United States, and his office maintains that the Global Fund 'was conceived to be an integral part of the administration's global strategy against the epidemic.'[27]

In practice, however, the United States has starved the Global Fund of resources by limiting its own contribution and by failing, as a result, to inspire others to give more. As noted above, in his 2003 State of the Union message, Bush set a five-year spending target for the Global Fund of just $1 billion, or $200 million per year. This is the amount the administration requested from Congress for the Fund in fiscal 2004 and 2005, but fortunately for Africa, Congress was more generous, providing more than twice as much in each year – $459 million and $435 million respectively. In the face of congressional support for the Fund, the administration grudgingly raised its request to $300 million for fiscal 2006, and Congress again responded more generously, appropriating $544.5 million. The administration requested $300 million again for fiscal 2007 and the same amount for 2008.

Even though there was stronger support for the Global Fund in Congress than in the administration, the amounts appropriated were far less than the $1.2 billion that the Senate voted to authorize for the Fund in 2004 in its version of H.R. 2069. In May 2003, Congress enacted Public Law 108-25 (P.L. 108-25), an updated version of H.R. 2069, and entitled the United States Leadership Against HIV/AIDS, Tuberculosis, and Malaria Act of 2003. The legislation had been rewritten to authorize the President's PEPFAR proposal, but it also authorized $1 billion for the Global Fund in 2004, clearly indicating where congressional sentiments on the Fund lay at that time. Before foreign assistance funds can be provided for a program, however, they must not only be authorized but also appropriated through legislation passing through appropriations committees. These committees must balance competing spending priorities and keep spending within the budget limit set at the beginning of the appropriations process for foreign operations. As a result of this process, Congress has never provided the amounts for the Global Fund that it has indicated in authorizing legislation it would like to give.

As the November 2006 congressional elections approached, some on the Christian right tried to drag the Global Fund into the political arena, potentially damaging its support in Congress. James Dobson, head of the fundamentalist Christian organization Focus on the Family, and representatives of twenty-nine like-minded organizations, wrote to members of Congress complaining of the Global Fund's support for condom distribution and its alleged 'near exclusion' of abstinence and faithfulness programs.[28] Dobson reportedly said that the Fund supports 'legalized prostitution and all kinds of wickedness around the world.'[29] Global Fund supporters quickly refuted Dobson's charges[30] and pointed out that it enjoys strong support from many others in the religious community, but the fundamentalist challenge posed a new element of risk for the Fund in Congress. How firmly the administration would defend the Fund, if it should become a 'hot button' issue among religious conservatives, remained to be seen. The Democratic Party victory in the elections themselves, however, likely improved the Fund's prospects for support in Congress.

Limited US contributions are hamstringing Global Fund operations. The Fund estimated that it needed $3.3 billion in 2006 and 2007 to cover the grants it has already promised through the end of 2007. In addition, it is seeking $3.7 billion, for a total of $7 billion to make new grants.[31] At the 2005 London pledging conference, donors offered just $3.7 billion, leaving little room for any expansion of the Global Fund program. In 2003, there was a sense in Congress that other countries weren't doing their fair share to support the Global Fund, and provisions were enacted limiting the US contribution to 33 per cent of all contributions in a given year.[32] If Congress regards one-third as America's 'fair share,' then the United States ought to be providing a total of $2.3 billion to the Global Fund in 2006 and 2007 – representing one-third of the Global Fund's estimated need. Instead, the 2006 congressional appropriation and the 2007 administration request total just $844.5 million. Congress will likely increase the 2007 amount somewhat, but the total US contribution will be far less than the $2.3 billion fair share of the Global Fund's need. A fair share contribution based on the Global Fund's need would be a leadership contribution, commensurate with US responsibilities in Africa and the world, and one that would challenge other donors to find the resources required to allow the Global Fund to do its job. As it is, the United States is failing even to provide one-third of actual contributions. The uninspiring $544.5 million appropriated in 2006 represents just 29 per cent of total contributions.

US officials make a number of arguments in defense of their treatment of the Fund, pointing out, for example, that the United States is contributing by far the largest share of resources going toward fighting the global pandemic overall, including both its Global Fund contribution and the bilateral PEPFAR program. A report issued by the Henry J. Kaiser Family Foundation in July 2005 found that the United States was providing 45.4 per cent of the funds committed by the G7 nations and the European Commission for international AIDS programs.[33] This is more than a fair share, administration sources argue, and if more is needed at the Global Fund it should come from other donors. The Kaiser study also pointed out, however, that when bilateral commitments and commitments to the Global Fund were adjusted for gross national income, the United States ranked third in funding international AIDS programs, behind Britain and Canada, although well ahead of France, Germany, and Japan.

UNAIDS estimates the total need for resources to fight AIDS in 2006 at $14.9 billion, whereas $8.9 billion seemed likely to be provided.[34] By 2008, the estimated resource need will reach $22 billion. A resource increase on this scale has to come in major portion through the Global Fund, and that will require a major increase in the US contribution. Congress has shown its support for much larger US contributions, but it will not be able to appropriate the needed funds until the administration takes the lead and comes forward with annual foreign assistance budget requests large enough to accommodate the increase.

Abstinence, condoms, and the prostitution pledge

The Bush administration expected PEPFAR to win it considerable credit among the public, activists, and friends of Africa generally, and more broadly in the world community. This is evident on the White House website, which is replete with 'fact sheets' and other documents boasting about PEPFAR and the contributions it is making.[35] Administration officials have tried to get maximum political mileage out of the program by successfully tagging it 'PEPFAR' and consistently referring to the initiative as the *President's* plan or *President Bush's* plan – even though PEPFAR was authorized by legislation (P.L. 108-25) called the '*United States* Leadership Act Against AIDS, Tuberculosis, and Malaria Act' and is paid for by the American people as a whole.

Yet winning credit for PEPFAR has proved difficult. The Iraq war, very much the administration's own doing, is partly at fault. Calling the world's attention to PEPFAR, however compassionate it may be, has not been easy, since the war has been the overarching draw on the world's attention since 2003 and the symbol of the administration's foreign policy. Direct appropriations for the Iraq war totaled $318.5 billion through fiscal 2006,[36] and this sum does not include a host of indirect costs, such as accelerated wear and tear on equipment, future military spending, and other unknown future costs, such as long-term care of the wounded. By the end of fiscal 2008, when President Bush's $15 billion, five-year AIDS pledge expires, PEPFAR will have been dwarfed by Iraq spending.

Meanwhile, PEPFAR's image has been damaged by the emphasis its prevention programs place on abstinence until marriage, its devaluation of the use of condoms as a prevention measure, and the anti-prostitution pledge it demands from contractors. These stances show that the administration is not willing to deploy the full arsenal of weapons it could use to fight the AIDS pandemic, but is instead holding back owing to ideological constraints and in deference to its conservative Christian base.

The damage from the abstinence issue arises in part from a misconception – although it is a misconception that officials have not been able to correct. Otherwise well-informed observers in Africa, the United States, and Europe commonly believe that one-third of all PEPFAR funds are being spent on promoting abstinence until marriage. Newspaper articles and editorials on the subject are usually more careful and note that one-third of *prevention* spending is devoted to abstinence programs, but few point out that as a result of guidance given by Congress in P.L. 108-25, just 20 per cent of PEPFAR resources go to prevention. Thus, spending for abstinence programs is set at 33 per cent of 20 per cent, or 6.6 per cent of total PEPFAR outlays. Yet this 6.6 per cent has been the subject of endless negative commentary, generally accusing the Bush administration of a naive and unenlightened view of the way the world works, and of interfering in the personal choices of Africans with respect to their intimate behavior. Stephen Lewis, speaking at the international AIDS conference in Toronto in August 2006, condemned the 'inordinate emphasis on abstinence at the expense of condoms as part of the prevention dimension of PEPFAR,' which he called 'incipient neocolonialism' and 'unacceptable.'[37]

In fact, the one-third requirement[38] comes from Congress, rather than the Bush White House, originating as an amendment proposed by Representative Joe Pitts to the House version of the legislation authorizing PEPFAR (H.R. 1298). Representative Pitts, a conservative Republican from southern Pennsylvania, describes himself on his website as born into 'a family of strong Christian faith,'[39] and his amendment may have helped the bill win support in Congress among conservatives of similar background and views. In general, like the administration, this group was highly impressed with the 'Abstain, Be Faithful, Use Condoms' (ABC) approach adopted by Yoweri Museveni's Uganda – and most especially with the AB portion of that rubric. ABC is applauded in the PEPFAR legislation, but Congress specifically stated that it was mentioning the components of ABC 'in order of priority.' In the Senate, there were doubts about the wisdom of Pitts's amendment, but in the interests of swift passage it was retained during the House–Senate conference on the bill.

In retrospect, the fact that P.L. 108-25 recommends just 20 per cent of PEPFAR spending for prevention will likely be seen as a much more important shortcoming than the one-third abstinence requirement. When PEPFAR was launched in 2004, the United States was spending one-third of its international AIDS funding on prevention, but by 2006 this had fallen back to 20 per cent in accordance with the congressional guidance.[40] Yet AIDS experts regard prevention as absolutely vital in stemming the spread of the disease and will mount an effort to end the 20 per cent restriction when the renewal of PEPFAR beyond 2008 comes up for debate. When the PEPFAR authorizing legislation was under consideration, however, there was a strong feeling that the United States should begin providing antiretroviral treatment to AIDS patients in Africa and elsewhere on a large scale and quickly. Hence, the bill specified that the lion's share of spending (55 per cent) should go toward treatment.

The Bush administration has never criticized the Pitts amendment, in deference to the views of its own conservative Christian supporters. Indeed, it has applied the requirement to PEPFAR prevention spending worldwide, despite a legal determination that it was required to do so only in the focus countries.[41] Moreover, administration officials rarely explain that the abstinence requirement affects just a small portion of PEPFAR spending. Mark Dybul did so at the Toronto AIDS conference,[42] but the message ought to be delivered at a higher level – by the Secretary of State or the President himself – in order to clarify an issue that is damaging PEPFAR's reputation. A clarification, however, might stir up controversy with Dobson and others on the Christian right, and this is something the administration wishes to avoid.

Administration efforts to implement the 33 per cent requirement have been the subject of a report by the Government Accountability Office (GAO), the US watchdog agency formerly known as the General Accounting Office. According to the GAO, PEPFAR officials have interpreted the congressional requirement fairly broadly to include AB activities generally, thus easing its impact. The requirement can be met through funding activities that encourage not only abstinence until marriage but also those that delay the onset of first sexual activity, promote faithfulness in marriage and monogamous relationships, and encourage the reduction in the number of sexual partners among sexually active unmarried persons.[43] Moreover, US missions in the field are allowed a certain flexibility in adapting the requirement to local conditions, and can even apply for exemptions.

Nonetheless, the administration's acquiescence to the Pitts amendment is important because it is part and parcel of an administration policy that is hostile to the use of condoms as a means of preventing the sexual transmission of HIV, except in limited circumstances. Prevention resources are scarce under the authorizing legislation, and apart from promoting abstinence at the 33 per cent level, they must be spread across a range of other vital activities, such as preventing mother-to-child transmission of HIV and assuring the safety of blood supplies. Devoting one-third of prevention funds to abstinence inevitably pushes condom programs farther down the list of priorities. Meanwhile, the administration has imposed an explicit set of restrictions on condom programs that reduce their scope and effectiveness. PEPFAR funds, for example, cannot be used to distribute condoms in schools, to promote the use of condoms among young people, or for any program that encourages condom use as the primary means of preventing the spread of HIV.[44]

Condoms are still a part of the US prevention program, and 176 million were shipped to the focus countries in Africa in 2005 alone.[45] But these were targeted at 'at-risk' populations, including commercial sex workers and those who have sex with an HIV-positive partner, rather than being made available to populations generally in heavily affected countries. Thus, a key weapon in the fight against AIDS is being under-utilized because of an ideological opposition to condoms within the administration and among its Christian conservative supporters. Damage is surely being done. Peter Piot, Executive Director of UNAIDS, noted in December 2005 that 'there is a huge shortfall of condoms in sub-Saharan Africa. There is no way to do effective prevention with just 4 condoms available annually for every African man!'[46] A Human Rights Watch report issued in March 2005 charged that abstinence-only programs funded in part by the United States in Uganda, where official opinion has now swung strongly against condoms, are providing misinformation about condoms, while at the same time depriving young people of information that could prove essential in helping them avoid infection.[47] Meanwhile, US policy on condoms is encouraging elements in Africa who are hostile to condoms and make irresponsible comments intended to discourage their use. First Lady Janet Museveni of Uganda, whose National Youth Forum has received PEPFAR funds, has suggested that condoms encourage promiscuity and cause genital warts.[48] Kenya's First Lady, Lucy Kibaki, has joined this chorus, blaming condoms for the spread of AIDS and telling schoolgirls in May 2006 that 'those still in school and colleges have no business having access to condoms.' For good measure, Kibaki added that 'sex is not for the youth.'[49]

Abstinence programs do have their place in prevention efforts; and as these programs have expanded, indications have emerged suggesting that some young people have changed their behavior patterns in ways that will protect them from HIV.[50] An authoritative consensus statement appearing in *The Lancet* in November 2004 endorsed the ABC approach, including abstinence programs as well as a range of other prevention activities, and was signed by a host of experts and advocates, including retired Anglican archbishop Desmond Tutu of South Africa and Paul Zeitz of the Global AIDS Alliance.[51] Such programs must, however, be implemented with a dose of common sense, in recognition of the reality that young people and others will sometimes need condoms in circumstances that would not win the approval of conservative Christians. As the consensus statement affirmed, 'all people should have accurate and complete information about different prevention options, including all three elements of the ABC approach.' PEPFAR will not make the contribution it could make to fighting AIDS, or win full credit for its contribution, until it follows this recommendation. The likelihood that the Bush administration will initiate a change in policy is remote because conservative Christian leaders remain opposed,[52] but

Congress may alter the constraining legislative provisions when it considers PEPFAR renewal.

A broader question is whether the ABC model is too confining and discourages the exploration or use of other types of prevention measures, such as the development of microbicides and vaccines, the prevention and treatment of other sexually transmitted infections that increase vulnerability to HIV, and research on male circumcision. PEPFAR is engaged in each of these areas, but they would have a higher profile in the public debate and in Congress if ABC were not emphasized as an exclusive formula for prevention success. The point is often made that the effectiveness of ABC is much reduced when women lack power in society, and more specifically the power to insist that their partners abstain from sexual contacts outside the relationship. President Bush, to his credit, has called attention to this problem by launching the 'Women's Justice and Empowerment Initiative in Africa,' aimed at enhancing legal protections for women and girls against sexual violence and abuse.[53] But the initiative is funded at just $55 million over three years and limited to four countries. More should be done, and it would be easier to do more if policymakers could break out of the ABC straitjacket.

The so-called 'prostitution pledge' is another PEPFAR requirement that suggests the Bush administration is allowing ideology and the concerns of its conservative Christian base to interfere with AIDS prevention efforts. P.L. 108-25 states that groups receiving PEPFAR funds must have an explicit policy stating their opposition to prostitution and sex trafficking. This provision was inserted by an amendment sponsored by Representative Chris Smith of New Jersey, a conservative Republican and one of the staunchest 'pro-life' (anti-abortion) members of Congress. The Global Fund and UN organizations were exempted from the provision by later legislation, but the Bush administration required that other foreign organizations receiving PEPFAR funds sign a pledge stating their opposition to such practices. The prostitution language in P.L. 108-25, though problematic in itself, did not explicitly demand a written pledge, and the administration might have sought to apply the law through informal enquiry and ordinary oversight, but chose not do so. The pledge requirement did not at first apply to US organizations because PEPFAR attorneys thought that it might interfere with their constitutional right to free speech. This changed on 9 June 2005, when the Bush administration informed even US-based non-governmental organizations and contractors that they must sign.

The pledge requirement drew protests from Save the Children, Care, and other charitable organizations[54] – not, of course, because they advocated prostitution but because they were concerned that the pledge stigmatized commercial sex work and could interfere with AIDS prevention efforts among sex workers. The impact of the pledge on Africa is not clear, since most reports of complications arising from it come from Brazil, India, Thailand, and Cambodia.[55] Judges in two federal courts ruled in May 2006 that the pledge requirement does indeed interfere with the free-speech rights of US-based organizations, and the status of the law for such groups remains uncertain pending appeal.

Conclusion

PEPFAR represents a major milestone in US relations with sub-Saharan Africa, if only because of the unprecedented volume of US resources it has brought to the region. Whether it will be judged a success in combating the pandemic remains to be seen. Experts do not expect current efforts, including PEPFAR, to be reflected in progress against the pandemic on a large scale for some time to come. To date, the major indicators of the pandemic's severity are not changing very much – in June 2006, UNAIDS was estimating 24.5 million people in the region were living with HIV and AIDS in 2005,[56] but this figure was within a possible range of

21.6 million to 27.4 million and hence no different from the 25 million estimate released in 2000. UNAIDS did report that new infections in Africa had apparently leveled off, but at a very high and unacceptable level of 2.7 million in 2005.

Nonetheless, it is clear that progress has been made in some areas. By June 2006, according to the World Health Organization, one million people in sub-Saharan Africa were receiving AIDS treatment with antiretroviral drugs.[57] This represents a tenfold increase over December 2003, although much remains to be done: only 23 per cent of those in need of treatment are receiving it. Declines in the prevalence of AIDS have been reported from Kenya, Zimbabwe, and urban areas of Burkina Faso,[58] although infection rates that had leveled off in some rural areas of Uganda seem to be climbing again.[59]

PEPFAR has certainly played a major role in this progress. According to the Office of the Global AIDS Coordinator, the program trained 35,000 African health workers in 2005; supported care for 2.9 million orphans, vulnerable children, and patients; and provided antiretrovirals to more than 246,000 women in 2004 and 2005 to prevent mother-to-child transmission of HIV.[60] In the critical area of treatment, which was of such great interest to Congress when it authorized the program, the Coordinator reported that PEPFAR reached 395,200 patients in 2005 with antiretroviral therapy. This estimate was perhaps a little vague in that it included 'upstream' support through capacity building and 'downstream' support at specific treatment sites, as well as an overlap of 214,000 patients worldwide whose treatment was also being supported in part by the Global Fund. Yet it was certain that PEPFAR was putting a major emphasis on treatment, as Congress intended when it authorized the program, and that it was making important progress. A report presented at the 2006 Toronto AIDS conference noted that in Zambia a major expansion of AIDS treatment had been accomplished in part through substantial PEPFAR funding, which allowed the large-scale purchase of antiretrovirals for as little as $300 per patient per year.[61]

Well before 1 October 2008 – and perhaps at some point during 2007 – Congress will consider proposals to reauthorize PEPFAR, or a successor program with a different name, for the years ahead. The controversies over the Global Fund, the abstinence until marriage emphasis, condoms, and the prostitution pledge have not helped PEPFAR's image, and it may be that Congress will conclude that a substantial portion of the program's resources should be devoted to other priorities, possibly including other health priorities. Those who seek a fairer and more just policy toward Africa will, however, see reauthorization as an opportunity to expand the program and correct its faults. Congress will be able, during the reauthorization process, to modify or do away with the restrictions, requirements, and recommendations that have kept the United States from making full use of all available weapons against the pandemic. Congress will also be able to make a strong statement in support of the Global Fund and to direct additional resources toward that worthy organization. Beyond 2008 the challenge for all who seek a better future for Africa will be to assure that resources for AIDS prevention, treatment, and care continue to expand. There will be no ethical alternative until that longed-for day when a cure is found or an effective vaccine can be administered to all in need.

4 | Democracy and human rights: strong rhetoric, few deeds

Support for democracy and human rights must be part of a fair and just Africa policy. In far too many African countries, citizens suffer under authoritarian and semi-authoritarian forms of rule that deprive them of the right to participate in government and limit their freedom of expression. This is an unacceptable situation on moral grounds, but also on the practical ground that transparency, good governance, and gains in income are far more likely in countries where the voices of the people can be heard and their wishes expressed through free and fair elections. The struggle for greater democracy in Africa, which intensified in the 1990s, has encountered numerous difficulties, including the weakness of civil society, the pervasiveness of patronage politics, the persistence of the 'big man' phenomenon, and social constraints on women's empowerment.[1] Nonetheless, it is a struggle that must continue, as is well recognized in Africa itself. Polls conducted in twelve countries by Afrobarometer, a consortium of African and US social scientists, show that more than 60 per cent of respondents prefer democracy to other forms of government, and they reject one-man rule, military rule, and one-party rule at levels of 70 per cent or more.[2]

In Iraq, the Bush administration neoconservatives have demonstrated their willingness to use the language of democracy and human rights to justify violent intervention and 'regime change.' Most of Africa need not fear this sort of American intervention, as will be noted below, simply because administration policymakers place the region so low on their foreign policy agenda relative to the Middle East and other regions. It ought to be perfectly possible, in any event, for the United States, as a concerned outside actor, to work toward furthering democracy and human rights in Africa by means that are wholly peaceful and constructive. Indeed, the United States has programs that are undertaking the hard work of promoting democracy in Africa in just this way. Both the US Agency for International Development and the National Endowment for Democracy are engaged in efforts to strengthen parliaments, boost civil society organizations, and encourage free and fair elections. But these programs are funded at modest levels and are making limited headway. They merit much stronger support from the administration.

Unfortunately, administration democracy policy in Africa has been marred by a damaging gap between a rhetoric that praises democracy in evangelical tones and an actual policy that overlooks violations of democratic principles and even pursues cooperative relations with anti-democratic regimes. Partly this results from the demands placed on US foreign policy resources by the administration's Middle East commitments, and the low value placed on Africa as a US foreign policy focus – a phenomenon characteristic not only of the Bush administration but also of its predecessors. The Bush administration may be in favor of democracy in Zimbabwe, for example, but the resources it is willing to devote to promoting democracy there are minimal. The administration's concerns over Africa as a growing energy supplier, as well as its conception of the way in which the Global War on Terror should be fought, are also key constraints on democracy advocacy. These concerns and their impact on US policy are given fuller attention in a later chapter. The point to be argued in the conclusion to this chapter is that the United States could easily afford to protect its energy and security interests in Africa while at the same time standing forward as a supporter and advocate of democracy and human rights.

The rhetoric/reality gap

The George W. Bush administration has proclaimed its support for democracy and human rights around the world, including Africa, in terms suitable to a crusade. In his Second Inaugural Address, delivered on 20 January 2005, the President said that

> We are led, by events and common sense, to one conclusion: The survival of liberty in our land increasingly depends on the success of liberty in other lands. The best hope for peace in our world is the expansion of freedom in all the world.
>
> America's vital interests and our deepest beliefs are now one. From the day of our Founding, we have proclaimed that every man and woman on this earth has rights, and dignity, and matchless value, because they bear the image of the Maker of Heaven and earth. Across the generations we have proclaimed the imperative of self-government, because no one is fit to be a master, and no one deserves to be a slave. Advancing these ideals is the mission that created our Nation. It is the honorable achievement of our fathers. Now it is the urgent requirement of our nation's security, and the calling of our time.
>
> So it is the policy of the United States to seek and support the growth of democratic movements and institutions in every nation and culture, with the ultimate goal of ending tyranny in our world.

In his State of the Union message, delivered a few weeks later, Bush added that 'The road of Providence is uneven and unpredictable – yet we know where it leads: It leads to freedom.'

The President's views on democracy are based on a dubious proposition – that the survival of liberty in the United States itself depends on the expansion of democracy everywhere. If seriously pursued, this idea could lead to expenditures and commitments that would leave the US government and the American taxpayer exhausted. This danger is already evident in the Middle East, where the neoconservatives and their democracy rhetoric have held sway. Rather than portraying the furtherance of democracy and human rights in self-interested terms as essential to American survival, it would be far better to recognize and affirm that supporting democratic principles and advocating human rights are simply the right thing to do.

The President's statements on democracy and human rights are also problematic because of their lack of humility and their assertions of American exceptionalism. These tend to deprive US democracy policy of credibility in Africa and elsewhere. One need not be a student of American history to know that it cannot be read as the simple and straightforward advance of democracy and freedom, as the President would have it; but rather must be seen as a continuous struggle over freedom of expression, the right to vote, and other issues that is not yet complete.[3] Of course, the United States, through history, has made major contributions to the advance of democratic principles, but so have other Western countries, such as France and Britain – and like the United States they have often deviated strongly from the democratic path, not least in their relations with Africa. Meanwhile, many other countries, such as India and South Africa, have made major democratic contributions of their own.

The administration's own history and conduct also tend to discredit its rhetoric on democracy. It is no secret to anyone that the 2000 US election was decided by the Supreme Court and not at the polls, that prisoners are being held by the United States without charge and without trial at the Guantanamo naval base in Cuba, that US-held prisoners have been tortured in Iraq, and that the Iraq war itself was launched after intelligence information was manipulated to deceive members of Congress and the public. These realities are recognized in the world at large, as they are recognized in Africa.

Yet the rhetoric is unrelenting. Policymakers have taken to

referring to the 'President's Freedom Agenda,' which is ostensibly at the heart of 'transformational diplomacy.' Secretary of State Rice describes transformational diplomacy as a way 'to build and sustain democratic, well-governed states that will respond to the needs of their people and conduct themselves responsibly in the international system.'[4] Speaking before the June 2006 annual meeting of the Southern Baptist Convention, Secretary Rice said that 'We stand for ideals that are greater than ourselves and we go into the world not to plunder but to protect, not to subjugate but to liberate, not as masters of others but as servants of freedom.'[5] In January 2006, Stephen Krasner, Director of Policy Planning at the State Department and a close associate of Rice, told a Washington meeting that the United States had a 'unique set of values,' was 'the most successful country that's ever existed,' and – more menacingly – possessed a 'level of hegemony that no other state has ever enjoyed.'[6]

Understandably, this manner of speaking about the Freedom Agenda gives rise to concerns that it is not really about democracy but simply a cover for US interference in the internal affairs of other countries, potentially including preventive war and attempts at regime change. This may indeed be what the Freedom Agenda has meant for Iraq, and might one day have meant for other countries in the Middle East if neoconservatives had not seen their power eclipsed by failures in Iraq and the outcome of the November 2006 congressional election. But what has the Freedom Agenda meant for Africa, and what does it portend? The answer must be 'very little.' The Bush administration has spent minimally and exerted only modest diplomatic effort in promoting democracy in Africa. But perhaps there is an upside. If the Freedom Agenda is a cover for regime change, most of Africa probably has little to fear, since, as this book has argued, neither neoconservatives nor realists among policymakers see the region as highly relevant to major US interests. The administration's determination to wage its Global War on Terror did persuade it to back Ethiopia's December 2006 intervention in Somalia to oust the Islamic Courts movement, and then to launch airstrikes against what it said were fleeing Islamist militants. Meanwhile, the Defense Department is pressing to expand its role in training and equipping armed forces in the Sahel/Sahara region. But in most instances, the risks and costs of US interventions to change regimes in Africa will be seen as prohibitive.

Democracy policy in practice

Despite its rhetoric in support of democracy and human rights, the Bush administration has repeatedly stepped away from opportunities to defend and promote democratic principles. Other interests that the administration values more highly have prevented it from taking a stronger stance in support of a cause it avowedly supports.

Zimbabwe Zimbabwe policy is a case in point. Robert Mugabe's oppressive regime there has perpetrated a long string of electoral abuses and human rights violations, culminating in 2005 in 'Operation Murambatsvina' – a removal campaign that saw 700,000 urban poor, suspected of supporting the opposition, rendered homeless. Impoverished Zimbabwe refugees have flooded South Africa, and Zimbabwe's reputation for violence and turmoil under Mugabe may have damaged prospects for growth and investment in the southern Africa region as a whole. The United States has been the leader in providing food aid and disaster relief to the Zimbabwe poor, who have borne the burden of Mugabe's disastrous policies, but US policy in support of democracy and human rights has not been effective.

US rhetoric on the Zimbabwe situation has been strong – during her Senate confirmation hearing in January 2005, Secretary of State Rice said that the country was one of six 'outposts of tyranny' and that the United States stood with the oppressed people there.[7] In June 2003, Colin Powell, her predecessor, had written in an op-ed column that Mugabe's time had 'come and gone.'[8] Christopher Dell, appointed US Ambassador to Zimbabwe in 2004, earned the wrath of the Mugabe regime through a series of remarkably frank addresses criticizing its abuses. Moreover, with European countries, the United States participates in 'targeted sanctions,' consisting of a travel ban on Zimbabwe government leaders, spouses, and associates, as well as a freeze on their assets.

Yet in practice the United States has never fully engaged on the issue of democracy and human rights in Zimbabwe. The underlying problem was signaled during a July 2003 joint press conference President Bush held in Pretoria with South Africa's President Thabo Mbeki. The President dodged a question on US policy toward Zimbabwe by saying that Mbeki 'is the point man on this important subject. He is working it very hard.'[9] Even in 2003, however, Mbeki's reluctance to come to grips with the Zimbabwe problem, despite the fact that Mugabe had created an economic and humanitarian disaster on South Africa's doorstep, was notorious. It has only become more so with the passing years. President Bush's decision to defer to Mbeki's leadership on democracy in Zimbabwe signaled that the United States, at the highest level, was determined to limit the diplomatic resources that would be devoted to the Zimbabwe situation. Tied down in a war in Iraq, the United States would let others deal with Zimbabwe, even if ineffectively.

Since the 'point man' policy was announced, the administration's Zimbabwe policy has not changed essentially, although US officials have expressed their frustration with the reluctance of Mbeki and the Southern African Development Community to pressure Mugabe.[10] The United States can do little more than it is currently doing, officials argue, until Africa is willing to take the lead – a stance that seems quite at odds with the administration's otherwise expansive view of America's role in the world. The divisions within Zimbabwe's opposition Movement for Democratic Change are also sometimes cited as limiting US options.

The argument that little more can be done received some endorsement in mid-2006 from the Brussels-based International Crisis Group, which argued that Mugabe was so entrenched that there was a 'relative paucity of sound policy options ... ' Nonetheless, the ICG called on the United States, the European Union, the Commonwealth, and the United Nations 'collectively to do a far better job calling public attention to the increasingly dire situation in Zimbabwe.'[11]

Surely more can be done than this. The list of prominent Zimbabweans subject to targeted sanctions now includes 128 people and thirty-three institutions, but a much wider net could be cast in cooperation with the European Union. The administration could use its voice with much greater effect to get the Zimbabwe situation on the agenda of the UN Security Council and to encourage African states to intensify their own diplomacy. US diplomats or perhaps a special envoy[12] could be deployed to persuade the Zimbabwe opposition of the importance of restoring unity, and to engage the governments of southern Africa to assure that they put the Zimbabwe issue at the top of their own agenda. They have an interest in doing so partly to demonstrate that their own commitment to good governance and development under the New Partnership for Africa's Development (NEPAD), an African initiative launched in 2001, is more than just rhetorical. Moreover, they share an interest with the United States in preventing the installation of a new dictatorship and possible regional destabilization upon Mugabe's demise.[13]

Mugabe's success in outmaneuvering his foreign critics is due in part to the close relationship he has forged with China, which provides both military and economic assistance, as well as investment. The conclusion to this volume will argue that the Bush administration has failed to develop an effective response to China's growing role in Africa generally, and that this is undermining its capacity for promoting democracy and human rights reforms. Zimbabwe is a case that cries out for intensive US discussions with China on what sort of involvement in Africa benefits Africa's people, and what does not.

Equatorial Guinea The seriousness of the administration in promoting democracy and human rights reforms in Africa generally came very much into question after Secretary Rice's 12 April 2006 meeting with another African dictator, Teodoro Obiang Nguema Mbasogo of Equatorial Guinea. Before going into closed session, Rice appeared publicly with Obiang and said, 'Thank you very much for your presence here. You are a good friend and we welcome you.' Yet as Senator Carl Levin, Democrat, of Michigan, pointed out in a subsequent letter to Rice,[14] 'Mr Obiang professes to support democracy, but he took power by a coup nearly thirty years ago, his opponents have been jailed and tortured, and his most recent 2002 election was condemned by the State Department as "marred by extensive fraud and intimidation." The State Department has been highly critical of his regime's human rights abuses, use of torture, and culture of corruption.' Levin went on to note that a 2004 investigation by the Senate Permanent Subcommittee on Investigations had detailed evidence showing that Obiang had 'personally profited from US oil companies operating in his country' and made large cash deposits in a US bank, including as much as $3 million deposited at one time. Ken Silverstein, an investigative reporter who had exposed Obiang's dealings earlier in the *Los Angeles Times*, pointed out that President Bush had issued a proclamation in 2004 barring corrupt foreign officials from coming to the United States – but even this could not stop the Obiang visit.[15]

The great suspicion was, of course, that in the case of Obiang, stated US objectives in supporting democracy and human rights had been overcome by an even stronger interest in Equatorial Guinea's oil. With oil reserves estimated at 1.77 billion barrels, and production expanding rapidly, Equatorial Guinea is regarded as one of the most promising oil producers in sub-Saharan Africa.[16] US oil firms, including ExxonMobil, are major players in the country's oil sector.

US officials defend the welcome given Obiang by noting that it provided the occasion for the signing of a Memorandum of Understanding (MOU) between USAID and Equatorial Guinea on the creation of a $15 million social development fund. According to the MOU, Equatorial Guinea will contribute the $15 million to USAID, which in turn will use it for programs in health, education, women's affairs, and the environment. To many, it seemed surreal to imagine that the US government would willingly take money from Obiang.

Policymakers, however, were upbeat about the arrangement, which gave them cover for justifying the warming of relations between the Bush administration and Obiang. USAID Administrator Randall Tobias said that 'Equatorial Guinea's decision to use government revenues for social development needs demonstrates visionary leadership and the potential of true transformation. This kind of agreement can serve as a model for future partnerships around the world, and USAID graciously accepts these resources.' Dr Cindy Courville, Special Assistant to the President and Senior Director for African Affairs at the National Security Council, added that 'The rewards for future generations will be great.'[17] These expectations seemed contrary to all that is known about Obiang and Equatorial Guinea. Inequities in the distribution of wealth in that country are extreme, despite the flow of oil wealth, and it ranks 121 out of 177 on the Human Development Index.[18] The State Department's own 2005 human rights report on Equatorial Guinea reported official corruption in all branches of government, the abridgement of citizens' right to change their government, and a lack of due process. The report also made note of restrictions on non-governmental organizations advocating human rights, violence and discrimination against women, and a host of other violations of democratic principles.[19] Social development in such a situation seemed unlikely, to say the least.

Meanwhile, Obiang busied himself helping his colleague, Robert Mugabe, evade US and other international pressures, such as they are, for reforms. Gasoline shortages due to economic mismanagement are a major source of public discontent in Zimbabwe, but in May 2006 Equatorial Guinea and Zimbabwe signed an energy agreement that will increase the flow of oil to the troubled southern African state.

Nonetheless, the US–Equatorial Guinea rapprochement went forward – and there was concern that it would not be confined to 'social development.' In a May 2006 letter to President Bush, Senator Joseph Biden, the senior Democrat on the Senate Foreign Relations Committee, complained that 'on May 5, you directed the Secretary of Defense to begin a military program with Equatorial Guinea under section 1206 of the National Defense Authorization Act for FY 2006.'[20] This legislation creates a special category of military assistance outside the normal aid programs which allows the provision of equipment, training, and supplies to build capacity for conducting counterterrorism operations or to participate in military or stability operations with US armed forces. The legislation also specifies that this assistance 'shall include elements that promote – (A) observance of and respect for human rights and fundamental freedoms; and (B) respect for legitimate civilian authority within that country.'[21] Policymakers concerned for political stability in Equatorial Guinea would no doubt be happy to fulfill condition (B), but condition (A) will prove problematic given the nature of the Obiang regime. Perhaps for this reason, as far as is publicly known, section 1206 military assistance to Equatorial

Guinea has not gone forward, although the government has been included in discussions on maritime safety and security in the Gulf of Guinea.[22] Moreover, $45,000 for Equatorial Guinea has been designated in the fiscal 2008 budget for International Military Education and Training (IMET, see below).

Gabon Nor has the administration's rhetoric on democracy and human rights stood in the way of cultivating cordial relations with Gabon, another country under authoritarian rule. The State Department's human rights report on Gabon highlights such issues as the limited ability of citizens to change their government; use of excessive force, including torture, on prisoners and detainees; violent dispersal of demonstrations; arbitrary arrest and detention; restrictions on freedom of the press, association, and movement; and widespread government corruption.[23] Yet on the White House website, there is a 'photo essay' showing President Bush smiling and shaking hands with Omar Bongo, Gabon's president since 1967, before a meeting between the two in May 2004.[24] In other photos, they chat comfortably before a fireplace in the Oval Office, and Mrs Bush converses with Mrs Bongo in the Yellow Room. No record was published of what was said between the two presidents, although a press release issued before the meeting said that President Bush was looking forward to discussing cooperation in the Global War on Terror and biodiversity in the Congo river basin, as well as the 'promotion of democracy.' Progress in that area has not been apparent in Gabon.

Perhaps the meeting was another instance in which democracy policy was overlooked because of oil, although the US Department of Energy reports that Gabon's petroleum production is declining and is expected to continue to do so in the years ahead. An alternative explanation has emerged from investigations of the activities of lobbyist Jack Abramoff, who has pled guilty in federal court to charges of fraud, tax evasion, and conspiracy to bribe public officials. In 2003, Abramoff had solicited a $9 million payment from Bongo in order to arrange a meeting with Bush.[25] No evidence has emerged indicating that a payment was actually made or that Abramoff played a role in setting up the 2004 meeting, which US officials described as routine. But whether routine or not, the fact that the meeting occurred affirmed the administration's indifference to the domestic character of the Bongo regime.

International Criminal Court The administration's stance on the International Criminal Court (ICC) is another instance of a position that runs counter to stated policy in support of human rights. The Rome Statute establishing the ICC, which has power to try offenses involving genocide, crimes against humanity, and war crimes, came into force in 2002. The Clinton administration, concerned that US military personnel might fall under the jurisdiction of the ICC, had voted against the Rome Statute in 1998. President Clinton did finally sign the statute in 2000, although he said he would not submit it to the Senate for ratification until 'significant flaws' were remedied.[26] But at least the possibility of US participation remained open. In 2002, the Bush administration closed that door by informing the UN secretary-general that the United States did not intend to become a party to the treaty. The administration, contrary to any actual evidence, claims that the ICC is an 'institution of unchecked power,' which might undertake 'politically motivated prosecutions.'[27]

The US stance weakens the ICC, and this is harmful to Africa because the new body is the first permanent, global court with power to try individuals for some of the gravest human rights violations.[28] Moreover, several African states have been directly affected by legislation passed by the Republican-controlled Congress and signed into law by President Bush with the intention of pressuring foreign countries into pledging not to extradite US citizens for trial before the ICC. Under the law, countries cannot receive US military assistance or aid through the Economic Support Fund (ESF) unless they sign so-called 'Article 98' agreements, committing them to the non-extradition of Americans. Article 98 of the Rome Statute states that the ICC may not proceed with a request for an extradition that is contrary to an international agreement a country has entered into.[29]

Most sub-Saharan recipients of military and ESF aid succumbed to heavy-handed US pressure for Article 98 agreements, but six refused to sign: Kenya, Mali, Namibia, Niger, South Africa, and Tanzania.[30] In most instances, the financial losses resulting from the suspension of US aid were small since they primarily involved the International Military Education and Training (IMET) program. This program provides training to small groups of soldiers from nearly all sub-Saharan countries each year. The loss of aid was not insignificant, however, since the program can serve as an important vehicle for the professionalization of the military.

A movement soon built among more pragmatic US policymakers to halt the aid suspensions, not because this would be the fair and just thing to do, but because they believed the policy was undercutting Pentagon efforts to pursue the Global War on Terror, particularly with respect to Mali, Niger, and Kenya. Secretary of State Rice said that cutting off aid in such instances is 'sort of the same as shooting ourselves in the foot.'[31] Some also worried that cutting off military aid and training was helping China increase its influence with African armed forces. Rarely mentioned was the fact that Congress had given the President power to waive the aid cutoffs if he determined that doing so was in the national interest. On 2 October 2006, President Bush did finally exercise his waiver authority with respect to IMET assistance,[32] but South Africa has reportedly lost several million dollars in other military aid, and Kenya's losses could exceed $30 million for 2005 and 2006. This would include more than $15 million in ESF aid intended for programs in agriculture and the environment, economic growth, and democracy and governance.

This list of instances in which the policies of the Bush administration in Africa run counter to a commitment to democratic principles and human rights could be extended. Aspects of policy toward Liberia and Darfur fit the case quite well and are discussed in a later chapter.

Democracy promotion programs

The US government does have channels through which it seeks to promote democracy in sub-Saharan Africa. These are modest but are making a genuine contribution to strengthening civil society organizations, political parties, and parliaments around Africa. The US Agency for International Development is the principal vehicle, primarily through the Development Assistance program known as Democracy and Governance (D&G). D&G assistance aims at 'strengthening the rule of law and respect for human rights,' 'promoting more genuine and competitive elections and political processes,' encouraging 'increased development of a politically active civil society,' and promoting 'more transparent and accountable governance.'[33] In addition, the United States funds the National Endowment for Democracy (NED), founded during the Reagan administration, which is legally established as a private, non-profit organization even though nearly all of its income – 99 per cent in 2004 – comes from the US government. NED states that its objective is 'to strengthen democratic institutions around the world through nongovernmental efforts,'[34] and it does appear to operate with considerable autonomy. Nonetheless, its largest programs are in the countries that are of most interest to the US government, and it must pay some heed to the wishes of Congress, which provides its funds through the appropriations process. Beyond USAID and NED programs, officials maintain that the administration is promoting democracy through the efforts of its diplomats.

The USAID democracy program, though valuable, has some obvious shortcomings – a limited and narrowing focus, and a limited and declining budget. Using funds drawn from the Development Assistance account and the Economic Support Fund, the administration plans to spend about $171 million to support programs aimed at fulfilling an objective it calls 'Governing Justly and Democratically' in fiscal 2007, down from about $183 million in 2006. Spending is heavily focused on southern Sudan, Nigeria, and Liberia – and to a lesser degree on Angola, Rwanda, and Sierra Leone – leaving little for advancing democracy elsewhere. Expectations of a program of this limited scale must be modest, although the activities supported are worthwhile in themselves – technical assistance to strengthen national, state, and local elections commissions in Nigeria, for example; assistance and training to civil society organizations in several countries; and assistance to establish legal aid and victims abuse centers in Liberia.

NED has drawn criticism over the years both from libertarians, who see it as a 'loose cannon' using US taxpayer funds for political purposes overseas without proper oversight from Congress,[35] and from the left, where many regard it as a vehicle for supporting center and right-wing parties that are favorable to the United States.[36] That this happened in Venezuela and Haiti seems well substantiated,[37] but in sub-Saharan Africa partisanship does not appear to be a problem. Overall spending by NED in sub-Saharan Africa is quite small – about $10 million in 2005 – but the Bush administration looks with favor on the work of NED and its 2005 spending represented a considerable increase from the $4.5 million spent in 2002.[38] Most NED grants are in the $20,000–$60,000 range, and in 2005 it was supporting nearly 160 organizations and projects in twenty-eight countries. Its heaviest engagement was in the Democratic Republic of Congo, where it was backing human rights groups and women's advocacy organizations, as well as projects focused on promoting ethnic tolerance, reconciliation, and civic education. NED was also heavily involved, with similar sorts of projects, in Nigeria and Liberia. While USAID confines its activities in Sudan to the south, NED has made small grants to groups outside that region, including $25,000 in 2005 to the Sudan Inter-Religious Council, which investigates violations of religious freedom and holds forums for young Christians and Muslims on religious freedom. NED has also provided funds to civil society organizations and the national elections commission in Somaliland, the self-declared independent state in northwest Somalia. Somaliland has not won international recognition, but it is respected for the quality of its governance. Several groups in Somalia itself also received NED funds.

NED passes a portion of the funds provided by Congress on to the International Republican Institute (IRI) and the National Democratic Institute for International Affairs (NDI), which are governed by boards drawn respectively from the leadership of the Republican and Democratic parties. NDI reports that it is currently active in fourteen countries in sub-Saharan Africa, while IRI is active in eleven. Their projects have included work with civil society organizations engaged in civic education and elections monitoring, and both are involved in programs designed to make parliaments more effective. Both also have offered forums, workshops, and other technical assistance for political party strengthening, offered to all parties on a non-partisan basis.

These democracy promotion programs have provoked surprisingly little negative reaction from African governments. Prime Minister Meles Zenawi of Ethiopia did take great offense at the arrival of NDI and IRI representatives in his country at the beginning of 2005. They had come, along with staff of the

International Foundation for Electoral Systems (IFES), to begin training and civic education programs in preparation for the May parliamentary elections, but were summarily expelled on 30 March. Meles told a TV audience that 'there is not going to be a "Rose Revolution" or a "Green Revolution" or any color revolution in Ethiopia after the election,' referring to democratic upheavals in Georgia, Uzbekistan, and elsewhere.[39] But NED remains active in Zimbabwe, despite President Mugabe's tirades against foreign NGOs, where it is helping Zimbabwe Lawyers for Human Rights, the Federation of African Media Women, and other groups. While these programs may lack immediate effect in promoting democracy and human rights in Zimbabwe, they could enhance the prospects for democratic change in the post-Mugabe era.

As noted above, US officials also maintain that US diplomacy is making a contribution to promoting democracy in Africa, but the results are mixed. In November 2005, the US Director of National Intelligence, John Negroponte, warned against a change in the Nigerian constitution to allow President Olusegun Obasanjo to seek a third term, citing potential instability and a possible threat to US oil supplies. Other officials expressed their opposition as well. Obasanjo went ahead with the third-term drive nonetheless, only to be thwarted by the Nigerian National Assembly rather than by international pressure. Still, some credit US quiet diplomacy outside public channels with contributing to Obasanjo's decision not to challenge the Assembly. After Obasanjo agreed to accept the Assembly's decision, the US embassy in Abuja issued a statement congratulating him on his approach.[40]

The United States also reacted with quiet diplomacy to the violence and allegations of fraud following the May 2005 parliamentary elections in Ethiopia.[41] Here, it is difficult to discern an impact, although US officials claim that diplomats, in communication with both the government and the opposition, helped calm the situation. For months previously, however, while Ethiopian politics were in turmoil, the United States had no ambassador in this critical country, and it was unable to prevent the expulsion of the NDI, IRI, and IFES representatives. In the words of Terrence Lyons, a long-time observer of the Ethiopian situation, US diplomacy reflected 'a lack of necessary high-level concern for the crisis ... '[42] Quiet diplomacy has its role, since a more outspoken approach can provoke a counterproductive hardening of attitudes – but at the same time, it can represent the easy path and bring no real gains for democracy. The value US officials placed on Nigeria's oil and Meles's success to date in keeping Ethiopia stable in a region regarded as important to the Global War on Terror argued against a more outspoken approach.

Conclusion

The Bush administration's crusading rhetoric in support of democracy and human rights in Africa and the wider world has been undercut by its own actions and policies on Iraq. The readiness with which US democracy policy can be dismissed by critics as hypocritical is particularly unfortunate because the United States does support constructive programs that are strengthening African democratic institutions, including civil society and human rights organizations, as well as parliaments. Funding for these efforts should be expanded.

Meanwhile, the administration could try to ameliorate the impression of hypocrisy in US democracy policy by toning down the rhetoric and adopting a more modest approach that acknowledges America's own shortcomings, as has been suggested by *Washington Post* editorialist Sebastian Mallaby.[43] Modulation of tone and humility of approach have not, however, been characteristic of the Bush administration to date. Even better would be a modification of the behavior that has called US democracy and human rights policy into question. America's reputation as a defender of human rights would be enhanced, for example, if it became an advocate for the International Criminal Court rather than a detractor.

Africa's oil supplies are important to the United States, but this does not require that the United States befriend authoritarian rulers in oil-producing states. The likes of Teodoro Obiang Nguema Mbasogo or Omar Bongo, dependent on oil revenues for survival, are not in a position to cut off exports to the United States. Moreover, African producers with offshore reserves will need US and other Western technology for deep-sea drilling for years to come. US policymakers might feel freer in dealing with repressive regimes in oil-producing countries if the United States had an effective energy independence program at home, as a later chapter will argue. But even so, the United States can afford to show more leadership on behalf of the cause of democracy in oil-rich countries, just as it can in Zimbabwe.

Dialogue with China must also be a component of US democracy policy. China may never become a supporter of democratization, but the United States and China share some common interests in issues related to democracy. Each suffers damage to its reputation when seen as supporting repressive regimes, and each will benefit if democratization ultimately contributes to development by strengthening governance and accountability.

5 | Conflict and peacekeeping: limited efforts, low priorities

The problem of armed conflict has eased somewhat in Africa in recent years, but violence continues to inflict insecurity, death, and displacement in Darfur, the eastern portion of the Democratic Republic of Congo (DRC), and Somalia. Incidents of armed violence and kidnapping are on the rise in Nigeria's oil-rich delta region, the Darfur conflict is spilling over into eastern Chad, and there are outbreaks from time to time in western Côte d'Ivoire, as well as the Central African Republic. Meanwhile, around the continent, there are many other tense situations that could easily explode into conflict. Some of these are in countries and regions that have barely had time to recover from past civil wars, such as southern Sudan, the broader DRC, Burundi, or Liberia. Other countries, with weak governments, legions of unemployed or underemployed, and myriad social, ethnic, and religious divisions, are also potentially susceptible to civil strife. The potential for cross-border wars is generally lower, but war could easily recur between Ethiopia and Eritrea, which battled indecisively over a border region of little value from 1998 until 2000. Ethiopia's December 2006 intervention in Somalia may have forestalled a new war over Somali irredentist claims in the Ogaden region of Ethiopia, but the long-term status of this potential conflict remains uncertain.

The fundamental responsibility for resolving conflicts, and for making peace when wars do break out, lies with Africa itself, and in fact several African governments and the African Union (AU) have made important contributions in facilitating negotiations and in peacekeeping. The AU mediated the ill-starrede 2006 peace agreement for Darfur, for example, where it has maintained a peace monitoring force since 2004. In 2003, the AU launched a peacekeeping operation in Burundi, later 'blue-hatted' as a UN force, with troops from South Africa, Ethiopia, and Mozambique. President Thabo Mbeki of South Africa and President Olusegun Obasanjo of Nigeria have been active, with other African leaders, in pursuing peace initiatives around the continent. Other examples of African engagement in promoting and maintaining peace could be cited. But Africa's capacity in these areas is limited, both financially and militarily. Africa needs the help of outsiders not only in peacekeeping itself – including training, intelligence, and deployment – but also with the complex diplomacy that is often required to persuade the participants in conflict to come to terms.

Offering generous assistance in resolving conflicts and in peacekeeping should be part of a fair and just Africa policy, primarily because such help can save lives and ease the suffering of the poor and homeless. The human toll of Africa's conflicts, after all, has been immense. Estimates of the number killed in Darfur range from 200,000 – the number used by US officials, including President Bush[1] – to 400,000,[2] used by advocates of stronger international action to end the fighting. An estimated 2 million are living as internally displaced persons in Darfur, and 234,000 are in Chad as refugees.[3] The conflict in northern Uganda, where a ceasefire took hold at least temporarily in 2006, created another population of 1.7 million internally displaced people.[4] A survey by the International Rescue Committee determined that there were 3.9 million excess deaths in the DRC due to conflict from 1998 through 2004.[5] Disruptions to healthcare systems, hunger and malnutrition, and increased child mortality – as well as rape, murder, and pillage – accompany African conflicts and add to the human misery. Beyond its immediate human cost, however, conflict has been a major factor in weakening Africa's investment climate and undermining prospects for growth. Conflict deters investment in the countries afflicted, and contributes to the all too widespread impression among potential investors that entire regions, or even Africa as a whole, are unstable.

There is ample reason, consequently, for the United States to do what it can to prevent conflict in Africa, to lead and facilitate efforts aimed at conflict resolution, and to try to ameliorate the human, social, and economic damage that conflict causes. This chapter assesses efforts of the Bush administration in these areas, while the next focuses on the administration's pursuit of America's own security interests in the region, specifically in connection with waging the Global War on Terror and protecting access to oil resources. The Bush administration has acknowledged the need for the United States to be engaged in preventing conflict and ameliorating its consequences. It has lent diplomatic aid to peace negotiations, contributed funds and some other resources to peacekeeping efforts, trained African peacekeepers, and provided assistance for humanitarian relief and conflict recovery. But with the exception of southern Sudan, where the administration's evangelical supporters took a keen interest, these efforts have been limited, both in terms of the priority they have been given in overall US foreign policy and in terms of resource commitment. Much more can and should be done.

The problem of conflict in Africa is intimately tied to the lack of democracy in many countries, poor governance, human rights violations, and the slow pace of development. As seen in earlier chapters, Bush administration policy has failed to address these issues adequately and consistently around the continent. Armed conflict often arises where governments are weak and unpopular, populations dissatisfied and disenfranchised, and unemployed youth forms a vast pool of potential recruits. Warlords can transform anger and poverty into armed political revolts characterized by organized looting, rape, murder, and theft. Policies that promote development, expand economic opportunity for all, and ease the grievances of oppressed or neglected minorities can change the underlying conditions that lead to wars.

At the very least, warlords should not be strengthened. In 2006, the Africa policy community in the United States learned with considerable shock that the Central Intelligence Agency had been providing payments to warlords in Somalia.[6] The amount of these payments was not made public, nor was it known whether other sorts of assistance had been provided as well; but the overwhelming consensus was that the United States ought to have been engaged in relief, rehabilitation, and state-building in Somalia rather than in assisting those whose interests lay in exactly the opposite direction. Critics were not assuaged by the assertions of policymakers that any payments were intended to persuade the warlords to turn over terror suspects.[7] The number of such suspects was thought to be few, and their presence would be far less a threat in a stable and recovering Somalia than in one kept in turmoil by warlords. The encouragement given to Ethiopia's intervention in Somalia, followed by US airstrikes against fleeing elements of the Islamic Courts Union, seemed unlikely to contribute to stabilizing the situation. While the administration offered to help fund the deployment of an African Union peacekeeping force to Somalia, prospects that such a force would be large enough to be effective were remote. It seemed far more likely that Somalia would sink back into warlordism and urban guerrilla war.

Limited diplomatic efforts

President Bush's 6 September 2001 appointment of former senator John Danforth as special envoy to 'lead the search for peace in Sudan'[8] was something of a masterstroke, but unfortunately one that was not repeated in the administration's dealings with other conflicts. First, the appointment proved critical in bringing about the north–south Comprehensive Peace Agreement (CPA), finally signed in January 2005, which put an end, at least for the time being, to a war that had raged for more than two decades. Second, it outflanked those Christian conservatives who would have preferred a policy of outright US backing for the Sudan People's Liberation Movement (SPLM) and its leader, the late John Garang. They saw the cause of the SPLM and Garang as a Christian cause that was protecting persecuted Christians in southern Sudan and had the potential for overthrowing the Islamist, Arab-oriented government in Khartoum. Mark Lacey of the *New York Times* observed after Garang's death that 'The religious dimension to the conflict captured the attention of many Christian congregations in the United States, leading to a wave of American sympathy for the rebellion. But many of his supporters glossed over Mr Garang's misdeeds. His rebel movement committed many human rights violations over the years, and opponents of Mr Garang often disappeared and were presumed dead.'[9]

Danforth, an ordained clergyman of the Episcopal Church of the United States (still part of Anglican communion despite growing strains with many African bishops and others), is a pragmatic, moderate Republican, who has deplored the polarizing effects of the rise of the Christian right on American politics.[10] He was supported in his work in southern Sudan by Walter Kansteiner, the Assistant Secretary of State for African Affairs at the time, who established a 'Sudan Programs Group' at the Department of State; and by then Secretary of State Colin Powell, who traveled to the region on two occasions. Powell held repeated conversations with Garang and Sudanese officials throughout the negotiations. President Bush himself telephoned Garang and Sudan's President Omar Bashir in December 2003, shortly before a key accord on wealth-sharing was signed.[11]

The sustained, four-year diplomatic effort to end the southern Sudan conflict contrasts with the episodic involvement of the United States in the conflict in Darfur, the vast, Texas-sized region of western Sudan. President Bush delayed for years in appointing a special envoy for Darfur, despite appeals that he do so. Congress upped the pressure in June 2006 by including $250,000 to fund a special envoy in the emergency supplemental appropriations for Iraq, Afghanistan, and hurricane recovery.[12] Yet the President waited until September to name Andrew Natsios, former Administrator of the US Agency for International Development, to the post. Although it came very late in the day, the appointment of Natsios was broadly welcomed by advocates of deeper US engagement in Darfur.[13] But whether Natsios had the diplomatic skills and the international stature – not to mention sufficient backing from the administration – to succeed in his position would not be known for some time to come.

A presidential special envoy has the potential for making a major contribution to the peaceful settlement of disputes. Able to stay in the region of conflict for extended periods, a special envoy can form relationships with leaders of the contending parties, and convey a sense to all concerned that the United States is treating the conflict as a priority matter worthy of continuous engagement. Nonetheless, the Bush administration has been parsimonious in appointing special envoys, evidently out of a concern that they can muddy lines of authority.[14] A special envoy can also tend to draw attention to situations, and add to pressures for action, that the executive branch would rather treat as low-priority matters. But special envoys are a valuable tool of diplomacy and should be appointed for each of Africa's major conflict situations.

Natsios bears the title 'Special Envoy for Sudan,' but the focus of his current duties is Darfur. One can only hope that he is also able to devote a significant portion of his time and attention to the implementation of the Comprehensive Peace Agreement in southern Sudan. This agreement contains a ticking time bomb in the form of a provision setting 2011 as the deadline for holding a referendum in the south on self-determination. Analysts look to this date with dread because sentiment in favor of independence is very strong in the south and because they expect the Khartoum government, as a result, to try to prevent the referendum from taking place or to intervene by force to nullify the result should independence be chosen. In either event, a renewal of the conflict would be almost inevitable. Khartoum, in their view, must be persuaded to implement the wealth-sharing and other provisions of the CPA fairly so that southerners come to perceive that they have a stake in remaining part of a united Sudan. If this cannot be achieved, Khartoum must be made to see that it has to permit an amicable separation or face unacceptable consequences. As it is, implementation of the CPA is lagging and the world's attention is directed elsewhere, including Darfur. Such a situation cries out for heightened US engagement.

The problems that can arise when a special envoy is lacking were made all too clear during May 2006, when then Deputy Secretary of State Robert Zoellick was dispatched to the AU-sponsored peace talks in Abuja, Nigeria. According to the *Washington Post*, Zoellick 'plunged' into the stalled negotiations, after arriving at 4:30 a.m.[15] The talks eventuated in the Darfur Peace Agreement (DPA), for which the administration can claim some credit, but it was an unsatisfactory agreement because only one of three Darfur rebel leaders signed. The sole signatory, Minni Arcua Minnawi, heads a faction of the Sudan Liberation Army (SLA) that is based among the expansive Zaghawa ethnic minority, about 8 per cent of the population in the area, rather than the Fur majority. According to reports, he has a reputation for abusive behavior[16] and was soon engaged in attacks on rival rebel leaders as well as their civilian supporters. In fairness, Zoellick had devoted considerable attention to Darfur over time, and visited the region itself in April 2005 and again in November. But if there had been a US special envoy at Abuja, with months or years of experience in working the issue and personally familiar with the rebel leaders – perhaps even trusted by them – a better result might have been obtained.

Zoellick, the highest-ranking official to devote sustained attention to the Darfur issue, left government not long after the DPA was concluded. Passed over as a candidate to be Secretary of the Treasury, he resigned from the State Department to take up a position with the Goldman Sachs investment firm.[17] In the months between his departure and the appointment of Natsios, the situation in Darfur deteriorated sharply. A special envoy working during this period might have made a major contribution to broadening the DPA, while also helping to investigate and prevent violations of the accord.

The case for deeper US diplomatic engagement in Darfur is all the more compelling because the US government has recognized what is occurring there as genocide. In September 2004, Secretary of State Powell told the Senate Foreign Relations Committee of his conclusion that 'genocide has been committed in Darfur and that the Government of Sudan and the Jingaweit [Janjaweed pro-government militia] bear responsibility – and that genocide may still be occurring.'[18] Powell's testimony followed the passage of concurrent resolutions in the House and Senate also declaring that the atrocities in Darfur constituted genocide,[19] and was followed in turn, nine months later, by a confirmation that genocide was occurring from President Bush himself.[20] Yet remarkably little diplomatic action followed initially from these statements. A recognition that genocide is occurring implies a need for immediate and utmost efforts to bring it to an end – that is why the Clinton administration was so maddeningly reluctant to acknowledge the Rwanda genocide. But Powell's statement resulted only in an appeal to the United Nations to investigate the situation. At a time when the United States should have been leading an international effort to relieve the suffering of the people of Darfur, the Powell approach only contributed to further delay. In January 2005, the UN investigators issued a report, which after a lengthy legal discussion concluded that the Sudanese government did not have a 'genocidal intent' since it was not, according to the report, seeking to annihilate the tribes of Darfur. Rather, investigators stated, the government and the Janjaweed were guilty of 'large scale war crimes' for attacks on civilians, burning down villages, and spreading terror.[21] The rebels opposing the government were also guilty of war crimes, but not on a large scale. Rather than precipitating decisive international action, this highly unsatisfactory report led only to a further referral – this time to the International Criminal Court.

A year and a half later, the ICC prosecutor did report that his investigation had documented thousands of alleged killings and that 'men perceived to be from the Fur, Massalit, and Zaghawa groups were deliberately targeted.' Moreover, perpetrators, according to eyewitnesses, had made such statements as 'we will kill all the blacks' and 'we will drive you out of this land.'[22] Clearly this is evidence of genocidal intent after all, although the prosecutor did not use that term. One day, when the ongoing ICC investigations conclude, some may be indicted for the war crimes in Darfur and brought to trial before the ICC – although it is far from clear that the government of Sudan would allow their extradition. An irony will be, if there are convictions, that justice will be served by an institution the Bush administration has opposed and sought to weaken. Meanwhile, however, the killing in Darfur has not been stopped by the ICC investigation; nor has it been affected by 'targeted sanctions' – the travel ban and assets freeze imposed by the UN at US instigation on a balanced slate of four individuals involved: one from the government, one from the Janjaweed, and leaders from two rebel groups. In 2006, the Bush administration finally began to press for the deployment of a United Nations peacekeeping force to Darfur, but as will be seen, its efforts were easily thwarted by the Sudanese government.

Beyond Sudan, Bush administration diplomacy on African conflict has not been any more active than that seen in most other administrations, and less active than that in the last years of the Clinton administration, when officials were trying to avoid another Rwanda-like disaster. President Bush's current Assistant Secretary of State for African Affairs, Jendayi Frazer, and her deputy, Don Yamamoto (later named Ambassador to Ethiopia), made visits and conducted other diplomatic efforts related to the conflicts in the Great Lakes region (DRC, Rwanda, Burundi, and Uganda) and the disputed Ethiopia–Eritrea border. But the Clinton administration had a special envoy for each of these – former member of Congress Howard Wolpe, who once served as chair of the House of Representatives Subcommittee on Africa, in the case of the Great Lakes, and former National Security Advisor Anthony Lake for the Ethiopia–Eritrea conflict. Sustained efforts of the sort they undertook have been lacking in the Bush era.

Parsimony in peacekeeping

The United States is making a large financial contribution to United Nations peacekeeping operations in sub-Saharan Africa, but apart from US support for the United Nations force in southern Sudan (United Nations Mission in Sudan/UNMIS), it is a contribution that is inadequate to the task. Table 5.1 shows the rapid growth in spending for UNMIS since 2005 through the 2007 budget request; contributions to most other operations will decline. The exception is the Darfur force, an African Union operation that received a major boost in spending in 2006. At the time of writing, the future of this force was highly uncertain. It

Table 5.1 US contributions to peacekeeping operations in sub-Saharan Africa (fiscal years, millions of current dollars)

	2002	2003	2004	2005	2006	2007R
UN Mission in Sierra Leone (UNAMSIL)	205.9	14.9	71.0	54.6	–	–
UN Operations in the Democratic Republic of the Congo (MONUC)	226.4	158.8	30.1	284.6	302.1	152.7
UN Mission in Ethiopia and Eritrea (UNMEE)	67.6	48.9	49.5	46.3	44.2	39.3
Burundi Operation (ONUB)			41.6	90.9	79.6	–
UN Mission in Liberia (UNMIL)			29.3	235.4	198.5	150.0
UN Mission in Sudan (UNMIS)				131.9	375.1	441.9
UN Operation in Côte d'Ivoire (UNOCI)			82.0	101.5	99.7	84.2
African Mission in Sudan (AMIS)			20.0	54.0	173.0	?
Total	499.9	222.6	323.5	999.2	1,272.2	868.1

Note: R = requested

could be blue-hatted, in which case spending would likely rise, or it could disappear altogether. Darfur spending in 2006 includes funding in emergency supplemental appropriations legislation enacted in June 2006, plus an additional amount temporarily re-programmed from the Global Peace Operations Initiative (GPOI), discussed below.[23]

In addition to its contributions to UN peacekeeping, the Bush administration has supported strengthening the peacekeeping and conflict management capabilities of the African Union (AU) and the Economic Community of West African States (ECOWAS), as well as other capacity-building efforts. These funds have come through the Africa Regional program of a budget account called 'Peacekeeping Operations' (PKO). Experts did not regard the $41 million provided for this program in fiscal 2006 as adequate either for helping Africa or for meeting US interests in reducing conflict in Africa.[24] The Bush administration slashed its 2007 request for the Africa Regional program to $4 million, however, in order to free up funds for post-conflict stabilization efforts in Sudan and Liberia – and for its Trans-Sahara Counterterrorism Initiative (TSCTI), discussed in the next chapter.

Since the 1990s, the United States has driven a hard bargain in negotiating with the United Nations on its contribution to overall UN peacekeeping expenses,[25] and this has limited what the United Nations can do in response to peacekeeping needs in Africa. The United States also bargains closely on its contributions to specific operations. The Council on Foreign Relations independent task force on Africa policy documented 'shortsighted' US efforts to restrain UN spending on peacekeeping for UNMIL in Liberia and MONUC in the DRC.[26] Under the 2007 budget, there is a sharp cut for MONUC even as the DRC undergoes continuing political uncertainty at the center and violence in the east. The United States has certain historical obligations in the DRC owing to its support over more than three decades for the repressive, one-man rule of Mobutu Sese Seko, which is the underlying cause of the country's current troubles. The reduction for UNMIL is also unfortunate, since Liberia has only barely emerged from long years of profound social trauma. There are historical obligations here as well.

Delay in Darfur The glacial pace at which the international community has moved toward the deployment of an effective international peacekeeping force in Darfur has been one of the most saddening stories in contemporary world politics. One expert on the region, Alex de Waal, has pointed out that 'Khartoum's perfidy and the SLA's divided and vacillating leadership are the main culprits'[27] in delaying help for the beleaguered people of Darfur. Yet at the same time, hesitant US leadership on the issue must bear a significant portion of the blame. The need for a much stronger peacekeeping force in the region, whether a UN force or an African force bolstered by a substantial United Nations component, became evident in 2004, when the violence escalated sharply and 70,000 deaths were reported.[28] But US policy at the time was to give very limited encouragement and support to AMIS. In September 2004, President Bush acknowledged that 'it is clear that only outside action can stop the killing,' but that such action should consist of 'an expanded African Union security force to prevent further bloodshed.'[29] In 2005, US air force planes flew in Rwandan troops to participate in the operation. But AMIS has never been more than a weak monitoring force that is unable to offer real protection to the people of Darfur.

Only in the first months of 2006 did President Bush begin to speak in vague terms of the possible deployment of a UN force to Darfur. In March, he said that he had called UN Secretary-General Kofi Annan earlier in the year and discussed converting the African Union force to a UN force under some sort of NATO leadership.[30] It was not until 8 May, after the signing of the DPA, that the President announced he was 'dispatching Secretary Rice to address the UN Security Council tomorrow. She's going to request a resolution that will accelerate the deployment of UN peacekeepers into Darfur.'[31] Clearly such a force was desperately needed in view of the suffering in the region. Moreover, the DPA had assigned AMIS immense tasks that were far beyond its capability, including the disarmament, by force if necessary, of armed groups that did not sign the agreement, and the disarmament and repatriation of groups from Chad that were in Darfur.

A Security Council resolution on 16 May 2006 set the planning process for a UN deployment in motion, but it was not until 31 August that the Security Council decided to deploy a force to Darfur to oversee implementation of the DPA and maintain peace.[32] The Bush administration and its ambassador to the United Nations, John Bolton, had pushed for passage of this resolution, but the entire process, including the Security Council's 'decision,' had an air of unreality about it, since prospects for early deployment of UN peacekeepers seemed remote. The principal obstacle was the refusal of Sudan to allow the United Nations into Darfur on grounds that such a deployment would infringe upon its sovereignty, represented a return to colonialism, and might be a cover for regime change. These claims were no doubt themselves a cover for the free hand Khartoum wanted to maintain in subduing Darfur and breaking the resistance by whatever means necessary. Moreover, it seemed likely that Sudan did not want a large, well-armed United Nations force in the country if it was planning, as many suspect it is, to sabotage the slated 2011 referendum on independence in southern Sudan.

The Bush administration, meanwhile, was proclaiming its leadership on the issue of a peacekeeping force, but seemed unable to make progress on actual deployment as the months dragged on and 2006 came to a close. The incentives for the administration to be engaged on the Darfur issue were strong.

Darfur had become something of a political issue in the United States as editorialists, other opinion leaders, and activists, including church-based activists, were demanding that something be done. The prize-winning columns of Nicholas Kristof in the *New York Times*, mentioned in the introductory chapter; the nationwide Save Darfur Coalition campaign <www.savedarfur.org>, with strong roots in the faith community; the writings and commentary of Professor Eric Reeves of Smith College, a tireless campaigner on behalf of Darfur's oppressed; and countless other efforts by individuals and groups were having a political impact. As a result, members of Congress, through hearings, bills, resolutions, and trips to the region, made it clear that the issue had become important to them and that action should be taken. In April 2006, five members of Congress were arrested in a protest against genocide in Darfur outside the Sudanese embassy in Washington.

The great question was whether the administration was trying to accommodate these political pressures by seeming to be engaged on Darfur without taking any real action. The incentives for inaction were also strong. The Bush administration was heavily focused on the Global War on Terror and the war in Iraq, which had a far higher place on the policy agenda than any humanitarian problem in Africa. US armed forces were spread thin, and the distraction of supporting or participating in operations related to Darfur would not be welcomed by military planners. Some worried that public opinion in the Middle East was already running strongly against the United States owing to the Iraq intervention and the absence of any effective policy on the Israel–Palestinian peace process. US participation in armed intervention in another Muslim country, it was feared, would place US Middle East interests in even greater jeopardy than was already the case. Finally, press reports indicated that the Sudanese government had been playing a supportive role for the United States in the

Global War on Terror by sharing intelligence information. Such cooperation would likely end in the event of a US–Khartoum confrontation over Darfur. The Central Intelligence Agency, according to reports, had flown Major General Salah Abdullah Gosh, the Sudanese chief of intelligence, to the United States for discussions in 2005, even though he was suspected of complicity in the Darfur violence.[33] According to retired US general Wesley Clark and John Prendergast of the International Crisis Group, these competing interests and the lack of a 'united front' within the US government on Darfur had contributed to the delay in developing a 'real policy to end atrocities, punish human rights violators, and create sustainable peace.'[34]

As the Darfur crisis continued without resolution, a sharp debate took place among experts in the United States over the course the Bush administration should pursue. Three Democrats with long experience in African affairs called for swift, US-led military action, including strikes at Sudanese airfields and a blockade of Port Sudan, through which Sudan exports its oil, to be followed by the entry of UN troops forcibly backed, if necessary, by the United States and NATO.[35] According to Susan Rice, Assistant Secretary of State for the region in the Clinton administration, Clinton National Security Advisor Anthony Lake, and Congressman Donald Payne, such action was essential to avert a second wave of genocide in Darfur. Representative Payne was later named to chair the House subcommittee responsible for African affairs in the Democratic Party-controlled Congress taking office in January 2007.

Alex de Waal, by contrast, was arguing that the idea of an international force fighting its way into Darfur was 'fantasy,' and called for a focus on strengthening AMIS instead.[36] J. Stephen Morrison, head of the Africa program at the Center for Strategic and International Studies in Washington, and Chester Crocker, President Reagan's Assistant Secretary for Africa, maintained that 'the United States has neither the stomach nor the means to force an international military intervention,' which in any case would jeopardize humanitarian relief operations in Darfur.[37] At the same time, they criticized the Bush administration for presenting the Sudanese government and its friends with a 'confused and contradictory agenda' that evidenced 'uneven high-level engagement and inadequate institutional capacity.' Morrison and Crocker urged that these problems be corrected and that Sudan be placed higher on the agenda of US–China relations. China, a close ally of Khartoum with a heavy investment in Sudan's oil industry, had been a major obstacle to stronger UN Security Council action on Darfur. Meanwhile, Nicholas Kristof was urging that the United States apply leverage not only on China but also on key Arab states to push the Sudanese regime to allow in UN peacekeepers.[38] He also sought financial sanctions against Sudanese leaders; the deployment of US, French, and UN peacekeepers to Chad and the Central African Republic, where Sudan was pursuing a policy of destabilization by supporting rebel groups; and a no-fly zone in Darfur to be enforced by US and French planes flying from a French base in Chad.

The ultimate resolution of this debate was uncertain. The use of US troops and aircraft in an effort to force entry of peacekeepers into Darfur was probably too much to expect from an administration so heavily focused on Iraq. The argument that such a role might inflame anti-American passions in the Middle East under current circumstances seemed a point well taken. According to a 2005 poll in eight African countries, a UN or African Union intervention would have far greater legitimacy in African eyes than intervention by a rich country.[39] Nonetheless, the creative ideas coming forward in the US policy debate over Darfur were making it clear that much more could be done in terms of pressuring the Sudanese government and laying the diplomatic groundwork for early deployment of an effective international peacekeeping force. When and if that deployment occurs, the United States should be generous in offering funds and logistical support.

More than two years after Secretary Powell had termed the situation in Darfur a genocide, however, there was little discernible movement, apart from the appointment of Natsios as special envoy, toward a more effective US policy on Darfur. In an August 2006 attempt to find an inexpensive way out of the Darfur conundrum, Assistant Secretary Frazer had visited Khartoum to offer a 'carrot' rather than a 'stick' – a meeting between President Bashir and President Bush on the sidelines of a UN General Assembly meeting if Bashir would agree to permit a UN force to enter Darfur. With US prestige at perhaps an all-time low in the Middle East, such a carrot was not much of an incentive for Bashir and might even have been seen as a negative. According to a press report, other carrots were implied in a letter Frazer conveyed from Bush to Bashir, but these promises also failed to persuade.[40]

In November 2006, UN officials said that Sudan had finally agreed in principle to permit a joint UN–African force to enter Darfur at some unspecified point in the future. China's ambassador to the United Nations was said to have convinced Khartoum that the UN had no hidden agenda.[41] After all of Khartoum's evasions in the past, however, this news was difficult to credit, particularly after Sudan's President Omar Bashir said that any suggestion that he had given permission for a joint force to enter Darfur was a 'lie.'[42] Natsios said that if Sudan did not give final consent by 1 January 2007, when the AMIS mandate was due to expire, the United States would resort to 'Plan B.'[43] Whether adopting Plan B, which was still awaited as this volume went to press, will mean that the United States makes a change in course, or perhaps one should say takes a course, in its Darfur policy remained to be seen.

Liberia The Bush administration's aversion to participation in peacekeeping in Africa was on display in Liberia in mid-2003, as rebels seeking the overthrow of President Charles Taylor, the notorious former warlord and regional troublemaker, advanced on Monrovia in a series of assaults dubbed World Wars I, II, and III by locals. In a just world, the United States would recognize that it has a special responsibility for the welfare of Liberia and its people. As noted in the Introduction, the country was launched by well-to-do Americans in the early nineteenth century as a colony for freed slaves – out of a mixture of humanitarian motives and a more dubious desire to cleanse the nation generally, and in particular the slave-holding American South, of the free black population. In later years, Liberia was neglected, in part because white American governments were reluctant to have dealings with a country governed by blacks. Injustices that sowed the seeds of later violence mounted as the former slaves and their descendants came to dominate the indigenous peoples and monopolize wealth and power. In World War II, the United States relied on Liberia for rubber and as a base for ferrying airplanes to the North African and European theaters; and during the cold war the country was the site of both a Voice of America transmitter and a US military navigation transmitter. This history might have led one to expect that the United States would have been on hand as a friend to Liberia and its people when the country fell into its time of troubles in the 1980s, but this was not the case. In 1985, the United States endorsed the election of the brutal and unbalanced dictator Sergeant Samuel Kanyon Doe as president. No real help was given to stem the violence during the 1989–96 Liberian civil war, nor when fighting resumed in 2000.

Perhaps too few Americans, in and out of government, were aware of the painful treatment meted out to Liberia by Washington over the generations. Yet as the death toll mounted into the hundreds in Monrovia in June and July 2003, and the number of displaced climbed into the tens of thousands, former president Jimmy Carter reminded them in a *New York Times* op-ed and called for the deployment of 2,000 American troops to help West African peacekeepers stabilize the capital. Princeton Lyman, a retired senior US diplomat at the Council on Foreign Relations, with long experience in Africa, appealed for 1,500–2,000 troops to be sent for a stay of nine to twelve months. Chester Crocker drew a parallel with British intervention in Sierra Leone to shore up UN peacekeepers, and said with respect to Liberia, 'It's our turn, it's our job.'[44]

In the end, the Bush administration put ashore 150 Marines for just ten days to help the West African force. Without question, the troops made a contribution in securing port facilities and stabilizing the capital as Charles Taylor fled into exile. In the process, they offered hope and encouragement to the people of Monrovia – although Liberians felt abandoned when the Marines withdrew.[45] Secretary of State Rice recalled these events as 'an example of US cooperation with African leadership,'[46] and the President's National Security Strategy Report stated that 'In Liberia, the United States led international efforts to restore peace and bolster security after vicious internal conflict.'[47] But in reality, the bare minimum was done.

Peacekeeping training The reluctance of the United States to allow its forces to participate in African peacekeeping is a major reason for the support it gives to training African peacekeepers. The Clinton administration launched the African Crisis Response Initiative in 1996 to train peacekeepers, and the program was revamped by the Bush administration as the African Crisis Operations Training Assistance (ACOTA) program in 2002. ACOTA was then made part of the Global Peace Operations Initiative (GPOI), launched by President Bush in 2004, which aims at training and equipping 75,000 peacekeepers worldwide by 2010, with a focus on Africa. ACOTA is the principal means by which GPOI is being implemented in Africa, and the program has been expanded to include Gabon, South Africa, and Zambia, with Nigeria joining in 2006.[48] Through 2005, the United States had spent $121 million training troops from nine African countries: Benin, Botswana, Ethiopia, Ghana, Kenya, Malawi, Mali, Mozambique, and Senegal.

GPOI, which was endorsed by leaders of the G8 at their June 2004 meeting in Sea Island, Georgia, has been a source of concern for many, particularly since the idea originated at the Department of Defense and was stoutly defended by Pentagon neo-conservatives Paul Wolfowitz, later named president of the World Bank, and Douglas Feith, now at Georgetown University. Skeptics have argued that GPOI is a scheme for training African recruits to fight in Iraq, Afghanistan, and other hot spots in the administration's Global War on Terror.[49] This concern seems exaggerated. It is true that once trained under GPOI, African soldiers could be sent to Iraq or Afghanistan if their governments decided to participate in operations there. Most African governments, however, particularly those of major peacekeeping participants, such as South Africa or Nigeria, would almost certainly not do so unless the operations became UN operations, which seems unlikely.

In reality, GPOI is designed to protect the Defense Department from demands that it make troops available to respond to African crises. As Wolfowitz told a House subcommittee in April 2004,[50] 'This is an initiative designed to train other countries' forces, so that when peacekeeping requirements come up, as they did recently in Liberia or as we're facing one in Haiti today, there are more capable foreign forces to draw on – so that we're not constantly turning to our military for tasks that could be performed by others.' Thus, GPOI is best seen as another manifestation of the low priority US planners place on Africa, and on some other places, such as Haiti, in contrast to regions they regard as more important, particularly the Middle East, where US forces have been deployed in large numbers.

Even though the motives that lie behind GPOI are self-interested, the program could serve a useful purpose. There is, after all, a shortage of trained and experienced African peacekeepers. The United Nations reports that something over 65,000 troops and military observers are currently serving in its peacekeeping operations around the world, including about 56,000 on duty in six sub-Saharan operations. Yet only seven sub-Saharan states rank among the top twenty providers of peacekeeping troops, together supplying about 22 per cent.[51] In such a situation, building Africa's peacekeeping capacity only makes sense.

Just how great a contribution GPOI might make to building capacity, however, is not clear. Funding is slated to total $660 million over five years, which is not a great deal even if Congress decides to provide the full amount. It appears, however, that Congress is not funding the program at the level sought by the administration. In 2005, GPOI launched a 'Beyond Africa' initiative, and the program is expanding into Latin America, Asia, and eastern Europe – potentially diluting the focus on Africa.

The evident shortfalls in funding for GPOI from Congress result in part from overall budget constraints, but also from doubts among some members and other observers about the effectiveness of ACOTA and GPOI. They worry that soldiers and officers trained under the programs may retire or be transferred; or may die or be incapacitated by AIDS or other diseases. Nor is there any guarantee that soldiers trained for peacekeeping will actually be deployed by their governments, or deployed in sufficient numbers, when the need arises.

Despite these reservations, it is worth noting that 11,000 sub-Saharan troops were trained under GPOI/ACOTA in 2005, and an estimated 14,000 in 2006. Six Senegalese battalions have been trained, and Senegal has recently deployed troops to AMIS

(Darfur), UNMIL (Liberia), and UNOCI (Côte d'Ivoire). Africa's leading providers of peacekeepers – Ethiopia, Ghana, Nigeria, South Africa, and Kenya – are participants in the program, which offers instruction in command and staff operations skills, peace support operations, and soldier skills. The program has recently been emphasizing a 'training the trainers' approach and provides some light, non-lethal equipment as well, such as uniforms, communications packages, and global positioning systems (GPS) equipment.[52] The Bush administration is often criticized for excessive unilateralism, but GPOI has a strong multilateral dimension. Consultations and information exchanges are conducted with other G8 donors that train peacekeepers, and the United States has made a $10 million contribution under GPOI to an Italian center that trains gendarme-type forces for peacekeeping and stabilization operations.[53]

Post-conflict recovery

The disarmament, demobilization, and reintegration (DDR) of combatants, together with development programs aimed at economic restoration and re-creating functioning societies, are fundamental to preventing new outbreaks of conflict. DDR is a key component of UN peacekeeping, and UN efforts in this area are held back by the close US bargaining on its contributions to peacekeeping noted above. The United States also contributes to post-conflict recovery through its bilateral assistance programs – but as is the case with US contributions for United Nations peacekeeping, the focus has been primarily on southern Sudan. Under the 2007 budget, US post-conflict assistance for southern Sudan would total $200 million, to be used for transforming the south's Sudan People's Liberation Army (SPLA) from a guerrilla army to a conventional fighting force; mine clearance; monitoring compliance with and implementation of the southern peace agreement; and supporting health and development projects. By contrast, bilateral recovery assistance in Liberia would total about $90 million, including $14.8 million in peacekeeping operations assistance for reforming and rebuilding the Liberian army. The DRC would receive just $35 million.

Conclusion

Under the Bush administration, the US contribution to ending conflict and supporting peacekeeping in sub-Saharan Africa has not been adequate to the need. The United States should expand its programs to promote development, democracy, and better governance in Africa in order to ease the underlying problems that lead to conflict. Diplomatic efforts to mediate and to promote negotiated settlements should be intensified, in part by reviving the practice of appointing special envoys to focus on critical conflict situations. Greater generosity in supporting UN and African peacekeeping operations would be well rewarded, not only because it would help Africa deal with destructive conflicts, but also because it would bring credit to the United States as a friend of peacekeeping rather than a skeptic and cost-cutter.

It is particularly important that the United States engage more fully in the Darfur crisis and adopt a consistent policy aimed at the early deployment of an effective international peacekeeping force. The United States should also expand its contribution to maintaining the peace and to reconstruction in Liberia, particularly in view of historic US obligations there. History and a concern for Africa's future also require a much stronger commitment to peacekeeping and reconstruction in the DRC. Finally, the United States must take care to avoid actions, as in the case of administration payments to Somali warlords, that might intensify conflict in the mistaken belief that doing so may somehow help in the struggle against terrorism.

6 | Threats to security: caution needed in the US response

The United States has two important national security interests in sub-Saharan Africa: possible terror threats that might emanate from the region and growing US dependence on African oil. These interests are real, but they have been of great concern among those who seek a fairer and more just Africa policy because of a fear that in pursuing them the United States will cause harm to the region. Many worry that US relations with Africa will come to be dominated by policies and programs that have a clear and direct relationship to narrow security concerns, rather than to broader, long-term efforts to reduce poverty, promote peace, and encourage respect for democratic principles and human rights. In the process, repressive regimes may be shored up, and military and police elements within African societies strengthened to a degree that could lead to repression and coups. Missteps and miscalculations may occur that will precipitate a backlash against the United States and regimes associated with it, causing lasting harm to the US–Africa relationship.

There is reason to be concerned that US policy toward sub-Saharan Africa is developing in ways that could have such consequences. Indeed, as shown in an earlier chapter, the US voice in support of democracy is already being muted with respect to oil-producing states. The emerging dominance of immediate security concerns in US policy toward Africa, however, is still in its early stages and is affecting primarily the Sahel, the Horn of Africa, and the Gulf of Guinea. Thoughtful people in government and in the wider policy-oriented community recognize the dangers and are arguing forcefully that the interests of the United States, and of Africa, are best served over the long term by policies that focus on creating a better life for the people of Africa. But the trend toward a security focus is very clear and if it goes too far, or, in the Muslim parts of Africa, comes to be perceived as part of an anti-Islamic crusade, the consequences for Africa and US relations with the region could be severe.

US security assistance initiatives

A major reason for concern over the trend of US Africa policy is the proliferation of US military and security assistance initiatives in the region. Most of these are only in their early stages but they have significant potential for expansion. One such initiative is the GPOI/ACOTA program, discussed in the previous chapter, which aims at training peacekeepers. This is a worthwhile goal; but the program is sometimes cited by analysts and policymakers as furthering US security interests as well. Friendly governments, after all, could deploy troops trained under GPOI/ACOTA in ways the United States might see as helpful in the Global War on Terror or in protecting access to oil.

The Pan Sahel Initiative (PSI) was launched in November 2002, when US officials visited Chad, Niger, Mauritania, and Mali, to discuss the provision of training and equipment intended to help these countries 'in detecting and responding to suspicious movement of people and goods across and within their borders ...'[1] PSI was not a major program. The International Crisis Group (ICG) describes the training provided as 'often rather mundane,' consisting of brief courses for groups of 130–150 soldiers in such basic skills as marksmanship and map reading.[2] Funding was minimal, totaling just over $8 million.[3]

While modest in its beginnings, however, the PSI subsequently evolved into an expanded and potentially much better financed program: the Trans-Sahara Counterterrorism Initiative (TSCTI), conceived in 2005. Nigeria and Senegal have been added to the

PSI countries as sub-Saharan participants, with Algeria, Morocco, and Tunisia joining as well, and Libya considered a potential future member. TSCTI began with limited startup funds, but in theory is to provide $100 million in assistance per year over five years from 2007. The actual funding situation for TSCTI in 2007 is unclear – so much so that House appropriators have asked for a report giving details[4] – and whether $100 million will be available cannot be determined on the basis of public budget documents. Some $30 million has been requested for the non-military sub-Saharan component,[5] but the costs of the military component are buried in large, operational budgets of the Department of Defense that do not specify spending on TSCTI.

According to policymakers, just 20–30 per cent of TSCTI will be strictly military in nature, but this is impossible to know with any certainty in view of the paucity of specific information. Some suspect that with the budget of the US Agency for International Development (USAID) constrained as the Defense Department's budget grows, the military component will turn out to be proportionally larger. USAID will use its TSCTI funds to promote economic development, strengthen civil society and local government, improve social service delivery, fund well-drilling, and support other non-military projects. The expectation is that this sort of aid will persuade local citizens and local governments to deny support and sanctuary to terrorist elements. If the Defense Department, with greater resources than USAID, should attempt to get involved in this sort of work, the results could prove counterproductive. The Department lacks skills and experience in development and humanitarian work, and the presence of US military personnel in civilian areas could provoke a backlash.

EACTI, the East Africa Counterterrorism Initiative, announced by President Bush in June 2003, was a $100 million program that aimed at improving counterterrorism capabilities in Kenya, Uganda, Tanzania, Djibouti, Eritrea, and Ethiopia. The program concluded in 2004, but it served as a model for other initiatives. It funded efforts to strengthen financial system monitoring, as well as police training; training for regional navies and coastal patrols; and improvements in communication, command, and control. The program also had a civilian component – funding teacher training in disadvantaged Muslim communities, for example.[6]

The Africa Coastal/Border Security Program got under way in 2005 with funds taken from other programs, but is slated to have $4 million of its own in 2007. Plans are still inchoate, but according to the Department of State the initiative 'may include' but is 'not limited to' twenty-three countries, among them Angola, Chad, Eritrea, Ethiopia, and Nigeria. Funds will support, but again are not limited to, training and equipment such as patrol vessels and vehicles, communications gear, night vision devices, and border monitors and sensors.[7] Budget documents reveal other planned 2007 security-related expenditures in Africa, including funds from the US Treasury Department to help countries combat terror financing activities, $2 million to help Ethiopia strengthen its counterterrorism capabilities, and $4 million for Djibouti to protect its borders and coast from terrorist activity.

The US European Command (EUCOM), which is based in Germany and has responsibility for US military activities in most of Africa, has been expanding its activities in the region. EUCOM provides personnel for the military component of TSCTI, conducts joint exercises with African armed forces, and fosters relationships between US National Guard units and African armed forces. 'Exercise Flintlock' in 2005 brought more than a thousand US military personnel to the Sahel for joint training with three thousand troops from Algeria, Senegal, Mauritania, Mali, Niger, and Chad.[8] EUCOM reports that its naval engagement in the Gulf of Guinea has 'increased exponentially,' rising from almost no 'ship days' in 2005 to 130 in 2005.[9] The Gulf of Guinea Guard is a EUCOM initiative intended to strengthen the capabilities of

West African navies in port and coastal security. EUCOM states that it does not seek bases in Africa, but 'Rather, with a diverse array of Forward Operating Sites (FOS) and Cooperative Security Locations (CSL), we will enhance regional training, assist partners in building capacity for counter-terrorism and counter-narcotics operations, and maintain contingency access for remote areas.'[10] The cost of this diverse array of EUCOM activities in Africa is not provided in publicly available budget documents.

The Combined Joint Task Force-Horn of Africa (CJTF-HOA), based in Djibouti, was established in 2002. The Horn of Africa is in the area of responsibility of the US Central Command, which controls US military activities in the Middle East, rather than EUCOM. Initially, CJTF-HOA was tasked with combating the movement of terrorists into Ethiopia, Eritrea, Sudan, Somalia, Kenya, and Yemen. Its mission has since evolved, and CJTF-HOA today maintains that it is not a 'direct action' military force conducting operations against enemy forces, but rather a military cooperation effort building local military capacity and seeking to improve underlying social conditions, principally in Kenya, Ethiopia, and Djibouti. Activities include not only military-to-military exchanges but also the construction of schools and hospitals, as well as medical and veterinary assistance.[11] As noted above, responsibility for civil projects of this sort would better be lodged with USAID, which has the experience needed but not the resources. According to its commander, CJTF-HOA has about fifteen hundred personnel based in Djibouti as well as five hundred others 'outside the wire' involved in projects.[12] Again, the costs of these activities cannot be determined on the basis of publicly available documents.

Threats and risks

Are all of these military and security assistance efforts justified by actual threats to US security interests in sub-Saharan Africa?

American officials and analysts argue forcefully that individuals and groups hostile to the United States and in many cases linked to the Al Qaeda terrorist organization are active in sub-Saharan Africa, particularly across the Sahel, in northern Nigeria, in Somalia, and down into East Africa. EUCOM and its commander, General James Jones of the US Marines, have taken the lead in envisioning the potential dangers. EUCOM officials refer regularly to 'asymmetric threats,' meaning in this case threats from non-state actors using unconventional means of warfare, arising in 'ungoverned areas' of Africa, particularly in the Sahel and Sahara, where 'another Afghanistan' might emerge.[13] According to General Jones, 'The growing use of the Trans-Sahara region in Africa by terrorists threatens the security of the United States and our European Allies.' African stability is a 'near term global strategic imperative,' Jones told Congress in March 2006, citing the Gulf of Guinea as a 'largely poorly governed maritime security region,' in addition to 'ungoverned pockets' in West Africa, and 'broad expanses of marginally governed areas' in the Sahel.[14]

These concerns have found their way into major US defense strategy documents. The Pentagon's February 2006 Quadrennial Defense Review (QDR) affirmed the tendency of terrorists to prey on 'ungoverned territories,' and in a chapter entitled 'Fighting the Long War,' noted 'emerging terrorist extremist threats' in western and northern Africa.[15] The President's own national security strategy, issued in March, stated that 'The United States recognizes that our security depends upon partnering with Africans to strengthen fragile and failing states and bring ungoverned areas under the control of effective democracies.'[16] These high-profile public documents do not mention African oil as a strategic priority, perhaps out of a concern that doing so would make US policy appear too self-interested. Oil policy is discussed further below, but it is worth noting here that EUCOM's General Jones, by contrast, has shown no reluctance in discussing oil as a strategic priority. He has testified that African oil could constitute '25–35% of US imports within the next decade,' compared to about 15 per cent today. Jones added that the region's petroleum is especially valuable because of its 'geo-strategic location' on Africa's west coast, 'allowing for rapid transit by sea to Western Europe and the United States.'[17]

Terror threats: finding the right policy balance It is difficult to assess the seriousness of the terror threat from Africa cited by officials in view of the highly classified nature of the information on which they base their assessments. The bombings of the US embassies in Nairobi and Dar es Salaam in 1998, as well as the 2002 attack on an Israeli-owned resort and passenger plane at Mombasa, make clear that terrorism in Africa is a genuine problem. In the Sahara/Sahel, the activities of an Algerian rebel group, the Salafist Group for Preaching and Combat (GSPC), have been a source of concern to US planners. Armed clashes involving the GSPC outside Algeria have been reported from time to time, although the details have always been murky. In 2004, a GSPC guerrilla known as el Para, thought to be responsible for the kidnapping of European tourists in Algeria in 2003, was captured in northern Chad and eventually returned to Algeria. El Para's force was reportedly attacked initially by Chadian troops trained under the PSI,[18] and he then fell into the hands of Chadian rebels who bargained over his eventual extradition to Algeria via Libya. But the details of this episode were shrouded in mystery, and el Para's significance as a terror threat was questioned.[19] The situation in the Sahel is perhaps best summed up by an influential report from the ICG, which argues that there are enough indications of a terrorist presence to 'justify caution and greater Western involvement.' 'However,' the report added, 'the Sahel is not a hotbed of terrorist activity.'[20]

In Somalia, despite the opprobrium surrounding covert US

assistance given to the warlords, US officials continued to insist that terrorists constitute a significant threat. According to the Assistant Secretary of State for Africa, Jendayi Frazer,

> Several violent terrorists have taken refuge in Somalia, including some of the individuals who perpetrated the 1998 bombings of two United States embassies in Dar es Salaam, Tanzania, and Nairobi, Kenya, as well as the 2002 attacks against an Israeli airliner and hotel in Mombasa, Kenya. These individuals – Abu Talha al Sudani, Fazul Abdullah Mohamed, and Saleh Ali Saleh Nabhan – pose an immediate threat to both Somali and international interests in the Horn of Africa ... We must therefore take strong measures to deny terrorists safe haven in Somalia – we must deny them the ability to plan and operate. [21]

US airstrikes in Somalia after Ethiopia's ouster of the Islamic Courts Union in early 2007 were evidently unsuccessful in killing these particular militants, but by then Frazer was enunciating a broader objective: ensuring that Islamists did not return to power in Mogadishu. The United States sought to ensure that extremist elements 'are not able to reconstitute themselves,' Frazer said, adding, 'They are on the run.'[22] No doubt there is enough of a terror threat in sub-Saharan Africa to merit a US response; but the case that it merits the proliferation and expansion of US security assistance and military programs currently under way, let alone airstrikes in Somalia, is not yet convincing. The few individuals cited by Frazer in Somalia, and whatever other threatening individuals Africa may harbor elsewhere, might better be dealt with by effective police work, intelligence gathering, and intelligence cooperation – which of course is already happening. A buildup, in Pentagon parlance, to 'fighting the long war' in 'ungoverned spaces' could prove to be an expensive diversion from this effort, which by its very nature is difficult and complex, and requires nuance and subtlety in its execution. What the yield of police and intelligence work may have been to date is not publicly known, but some reports suggest that there have been troubling, heavy-handed incidents. In mid-2003, a disturbing episode came to light involving five foreign suspects arrested in Malawi in what was said to be a joint US–Malawi operation. Despite a Malawi court injunction, they were reportedly flown to an unknown destination – Zimbabwe was disconcertingly mentioned – for interrogation before being released in Sudan.[23] In July 2006, an Algerian alleged that he had been expelled from Tanzania to Malawi in 2003, handed over to Americans, and flown to Afghanistan for prolonged, harsh interrogation before he too was released.[24]

In conducting its anti-terror activities in sub-Saharan Africa, the United States needs to proceed with great care and caution and observe legal norms, lest it provoke a backlash. Press accounts suggest that US aid to the warlords in Somalia may actually have provoked the Islamic Courts movement to act pre-emptively to seize Mogadishu, before its warlord foes became too powerful. According to a *Washington Post* account, the United States expanded its aid in the first months of 2006 in the mistaken belief that a small team of intelligence officers visiting in January had come under attack – whereas in fact they had merely happened to arrive in the midst of a clan dispute.[25] The Somali warlord episode, at a minimum, suggests a lack of information and understanding that allowed the United States to be manipulated by local forces for their own purposes, which were not related to the war on terror.

If small-scale, clandestine operations can go this wrong, the dangers inherent in larger efforts must be great indeed. Mali and Niger are fragile, easily destabilized democracies. Mauritania, under a military government once again following a 2005 coup, is slated for another democratic transition in 2007. These countries have been subject to long years of military and one-party rule in the past, and further military takeovers in the future are easily conceivable. In the circumstances, strengthening the military element unduly could prove destabilizing and a threat to promoting democracy and improved governance. The tribal, political, and religious forces at work across the Sahel are not well understood in Washington, increasing the risk of mistakes and incidents that could lead to a popular backlash against the American presence and the regimes that permitted it. The unpopularity among Muslims of US policies toward the Middle East could only add to the backlash.

The ICG has documented the regional complexities that contribute to the danger of miscalculation. These include the intimidating array of divisions among Muslims into Sufi, Wahhabi, and Tablighi movements, as well as the presence of numerous Islamic NGOs.[26] Mauritanian society is split between a ruling 'Moor' elite and impoverished African groups, Mali faces ongoing dissatisfaction (despite some recent progress toward reconciliation) among the Tuareg in the north, and Chad is dominated by a Zaghawa minority that many Chadians wish to overthrow. In the circumstances, the chances for the United States to blunder in counterproductive ways and/or to be manipulated by local forces are immense. While the risks of unintended consequences seem greatest in the Sahel at present, counterterrorism policies could tend to undermine US democracy and governance objectives in Ethiopia, Uganda, Kenya, and other countries as well.

In short, US policy in pursuit of its counterterror interests in sub-Saharan Africa may already be causing harm, and there is a grave risk that the harm will increase as counterterrorism programs expand. US officials maintain that they recognize the dangers, and that is why TSCTI, CJTF-HOA, and other efforts are placing such emphasis on economic development and humanitarian relief. But the Defense Department's vast resources and institutional imperatives could well lead to an unbalanced expansion of the military component. The Department clearly views Africa as a region where it will have a growing role, and this has helped EUCOM expand its involvement in the region. Now the Pentagon is moving forward with plans to create a separate 'Africa Command,'[27] ending the awkward division of responsibilities in Africa between EUCOM and Central Command. Some who are basically sympathetic to Africa and its needs favor this proposal because it would create a powerful new center of advocacy for greater US attention to Africa and increased expenditures on Africa programs. The risk that an Africa Command, with its own institutional imperatives, would accelerate the militarization of the US–Africa relationship is very high, however, and it is unreasonable to expect that its creation would contribute to a fairer and more just Africa policy.

Another reason to be concerned about the expanding military dimension in counterterrorism efforts in Africa is the continuing influence in conservative and neoconservative political circles of those who argue that the United States is at war with Islam or that such a war is coming. This way of thinking is greeted with dismay by responsible policymakers, as it should be, but it has the potential for contributing to serious problems for Africa and for the United States in the Muslim regions of Africa. Army Lieutenant General William G. 'Jerry' Boykin, famous for anti-Islamic remarks before church groups likening the war on terror to a war against Satan, remains in high Pentagon office as Deputy Undersecretary for Intelligence and Warfighting Support. Boykin once remarked that in fighting a Somali warlord in 1993, 'I knew my God was bigger than his. I knew that my God was a real God and his was an idol.'[28] Others are keeping up a steady drumbeat of commentary on the rise of Islamism in Africa, the supposed 'Talibanization' of Nigeria, and the threat posed by Islamists to 'persecuted Christians.'[29] President Bush himself, as noted in the Introduction, said in January 2006 that the United States is at war with 'radical Islam,' and in August 2006 he raised the rhetoric a notch by stating that 'this nation is at war with Islamic fascists.'[30] Senator Russell Feingold, a Democrat, noted that this term was offensive to Muslims,[31] who feel it defames the faith and its adherents as a whole. Many worried that its use by the President would further the cause of those who want to expand US military involvement in Muslim regions, including those in Africa. Remarks with religious overtones are generally avoided by policymakers at lower levels, and abhorred by most who participate in the ongoing Africa policy discussion in Washington and the wider US Africanist community. It cannot yet be said that the United States is on an anti-Muslim crusade – but one shudders to think of the possible consequences for US relations with Muslim Africa of another major terror attack in the United States itself. In that event, a drastic expansion in the US military role in sub-Saharan Africa might well occur – and if there were any hint of an African angle to the attack, it could prove unstoppable.

Threats to oil supplies As for the threat to US oil supplies from sub-Saharan Africa, the greatest concern for US analysts is Nigeria, the leading US African supplier, which provides about 1.1 million barrels per day or more than 8 per cent of US petroleum imports.[32] Despite the sense of alarm conveyed by General Jones, however, there is not yet a compelling case to be made for a general threat to the security of African oil, much of which comes from countries that seem to be politically stable for the time being. This has tended to restrain the growth of US military and security assistance initiatives related to oil to date, although pressure for expansion from within the defense community continues. At the same time, because of oil, the administration is cultivating relations with regimes that are neither transparent nor democratic, to the long-term detriment of US interests and Africa itself.

Concerns over Nigeria's future run deep. In 2005, the US

National Intelligence Council convened a panel of experts which famously concluded that there was a 'downside risk' of the 'outright collapse' of Nigeria over the next fifteen years, possibly as a result of a 'junior officer coup that could destabilize the country to the extent that open warfare breaks out in many places in a sustained manner.' If Nigeria should become a failed state, according to the panel, 'it could drag down a large part of the West African region.'[33]

Analysts are worried that the spread of Islamism in northern Nigeria could destabilize the country and note with alarm that Osama bin Laden has reportedly called on Nigerian Muslims to overthrow the 'apostate' regime in Abuja.[34] The growth of guerrilla movements in the oil-producing regions of southern Nigeria, which are not predominantly Muslim, is another concern. Some speculate that the Islamists and the guerrillas could form links that will pose an even more potent threat to Nigeria's oil exports. Nigerian offshore platforms were once thought secure, but these too have been attacked by rebels in speedboats and workers kidnapped.

In view of the importance of Nigerian oil to the United States, limited US efforts to bolster maritime security in the Gulf of Guinea are understandable, and it would hardly be surprising if a US program to provide coastal patrol craft and training should emerge. Surplus US Coast Guard tenders have already been transferred to the Nigerian navy.[35] But beyond these steps, it is difficult to see what further military measures might be taken. Any but the most minor US military presence in Nigeria, with its volatile mix of religious, ethnic, and economic tensions, could prove counterproductive in the extreme. This appears to be recognized by US planners, and the principal focus of US involvement in Nigeria is through the very large Nigerian PEPFAR program rather than through security assistance. Some assistance is also going to anti-corruption projects, strengthening state electoral commissions, boosting agricultural output, and education – and to aid in fighting drug trafficking and crime. This judicious approach might come under pressure in the event of a worsening of the security situation in the Niger delta region, increased piracy in the Gulf of Guinea, or a sharp escalation in petroleum prices.

In other African oil-producing countries, with the possible exception of Chad, there appears to be no immediate armed threat to oil facilities. Rather, the danger is that corruption and inequity in the distribution of oil wealth will, over the long term, lead to the sort of societal breakdown that now looms in southern Nigeria. That is why it is so important for the Bush administration to strengthen its support for transparency and governance – and to avoid the appearance of coddling corrupt regimes, as in Equatorial Guinea or Gabon. In the case of Chad, it appears that the administration has failed to hold the government's feet to the fire with respect to its once-vaunted pledge to commit the bulk of its oil revenues to poverty alleviation and development, and to a fund for future generations. Chad had agreed to these provisions in exchange for World Bank support for the development of oilfields in the south by an oil company consortium led by ExxonMobil and the construction of a pipeline to a port in Cameroon. In January 2006, the World Bank suspended its loans to Chad and froze the future generations fund after Chad enacted legislation abolishing the fund and upping the share of oil revenue going directly to the government without supervision to 30 per cent from 13.5 per cent.[36] Chad's move was widely seen as an attempt to secure money for unsupervised weapons purchases and for spending that would benefit the ruling elite. In April, however, the Bank agreed to a temporary arrangement allowing the government to keep its 30 per cent of revenue, but leaving the fate of the future generations fund unresolved. The *Boston Globe* reported that the Bank had backed away from a confrontation following the intervention of US diplomats 'acting on behalf of

US oil companies.'[37] Chad's president, Idris Deby, had threatened to shut down oil production and demanded $100 million from ExxonMobil to tide the government over the crisis.

A final agreement between the World Bank and Chad, announced in July 2006, committed the Chad government to devoting 70 per cent of all revenues, not just oil revenues, to poverty reduction, with any budget surpluses going to an economic stabilization fund.[38] This was seen as something of a recovery for advocates of development, but the fact is that the future generations fund is gone and the Deby regime has much larger unsupervised resources at its disposal than it had before. Pressure from the Bush administration for greater transparency and better governance in Chad and other oil-producing countries will likely remain muted in an era of tight oil supplies and high prices. The Bush administration could increase its freedom of action in dealing with African oil producers by reducing US dependence on imported oil. This could be accomplished through a substantially higher tax on gasoline, increased mileage standards for vehicles in the United States, and other measures that have been urged for years.[39] But this is an effort the administration has been unwilling to make.

Conclusion

In pursuing its security interests in sub-Saharan Africa, the United States can afford to be both more cautious in its military commitments and more generous in implementing a fair and just development policy. The threat of terrorism and threats to oil supplies are not so great as to require any major expansion of US military involvement, and if such expansion does occur, it could well prove counterproductive, provoking threats of the sort it was intended to prevent. The danger of miscalculation is high in view of limited American understanding of diverse and complex African societies. The emerging tendency to pull back on support for transparency and better governance in the interests of securing oil supplies should be reversed. Indeed, the United States should always be seen to be at the forefront in the pursuit of transparency and better governance around the continent, and it should give its full backing to international efforts aimed at the same objectives, such as the Extractive Industries Transparency Initiative (EITI).[40]

US security interests will be best protected where opportunities for employment, education, and healthcare are expanding, and poverty is being reduced. This requires that aid, trade, and development policy be at the fore, that democracy policy be consistent, that international peacekeeping efforts are fully supported, and conflict resolution initiatives are pursued resolutely.

The central problems facing Africa today, after all, do not lie in its 'ungoverned spaces,' but in its teeming cities and impoverished rural areas. Terror recruits are more likely to be found in Kenya's neglected coastal strip or the Lagos slums than in the Sahara. Repression and corruption in oil-producing states create the sort of instability that can endanger oil supplies over the long term, as is happening today in the Niger delta. US initiatives in countries with Muslim majorities or large Muslim minorities are going to face special challenges for the foreseeable future owing to the unpopularity of US policies in the Middle East. Extreme care must be taken in engaging with these societies in order not to provoke a backlash damaging to Africa and to US security interests.

7 | Beyond the Bush administration: toward a fairer and more just Africa policy

The United States ought to have a fairer and more just Africa policy. Its position as the world's wealthiest nation creates a special moral responsibility to do more to help Africa's poor. Moreover, the United States has an historical obligation to help Africa recover from the harm it has done in the past, not only during the era of slavery and the slave trade, but also during the cold war and the struggle for liberation in southern Africa, as well as through its trade policies. Disengagement is not an option, in part because of these obligations and in part because Africa's great current needs with respect to poverty, conflict, and health inevitably draw the attention of concerned Americans who demand that their government respond. In addition, economic and security interests increasingly bind the United States to Africa. It has been a thesis of this volume that these interests would best be served by an Africa policy that promotes African development and a better life for Africa's people.

The United States also needs a fairer and more just Africa policy because its image as an advocate of justice, democracy, human rights, and peace has been severely tarnished during the George W. Bush administration. This image always had flaws, but it was true enough to win the United States considerable respect around the world and even some affection. Now, as the US intelligence community recognized in an April 2006 National Intelligence Estimate (NIE), that image has been damaged to a degree that puts the United States itself at risk. In the Muslim world, according to the NIE, 'jihads' dedicated to the destruction of the United States and US interests are 'increasing in both number and geographic dispersion.' Elsewhere, 'Anti-US and anti-globalization sentiment is on the rise and fuelling other radical ideologies.'[1] A better Africa policy would offer the United States an opportunity to win back some of the respect and affection it has lost, and in so doing improve its own security.

The Bush administration deserves credit for launching its PEPFAR program and boosting aid levels to Africa, but in other areas, such as peacekeeping or supporting democratic principles and human rights, its efforts have fallen short of reasonable standards of justice and fairness. With its trade policies and double standards on democracy for leaders of oil-rich nations, it has done harm to the region.

The United States can do better than this. It should expand its development assistance programs in Africa, strengthen Africa's capacity for growth through new commitments to infrastructure projects and education, and pursue development objectives rather than political agendas with its assistance funds. It should adopt a trade policy that treats African farmers fairly. The United States should give full support to the Global Fund to Fight AIDS, Tuberculosis, and Malaria and work with other major donors to ensure that their contributions increase as well. The President's Emergency Plan for AIDS Relief should be renewed, of course, and its prevention component sharply expanded. The restrictions, requirements, and recommendations in the existing PEPFAR legislation, which have caused so much controversy and hampered the United States in responding to the AIDS pandemic, should be done away with.

The reputation of the United States as a defender of human rights and democratic principles will be difficult to restore, but a start could be made in Africa by expanding the democracy support programs that strengthen civil society and human rights organizations, as well as parliaments. A cessation of the pressure on African governments to sign Article 98 agreements exempting Americans from the jurisdiction of the International Criminal Court would help as well. Even better would be a fundamental reorientation of US policy toward the Court – from critic and detractor to advocate and supporter. The United States should be consistent in its encouragement of democratic regimes in Africa, and not befriend authoritarian governments simply because they happen to control petroleum assets.

To ease the burden armed conflict imposes on Africa, the United States should be more generous in its support of peacekeeping. It should show real leadership in the effort to resolve the crisis in Darfur – as well as other, similar crises when they arise in the future. Bilateral military relationships related to the Global War on Terror or protecting oil supplies should be pursued with the utmost caution. The presence of US military personnel and close associations between the Pentagon and African armed forces run the risk of provoking reactions that will be harmful to Africa and to the United States. US security interests in Africa are more likely to be furthered by policies that promote development and widen economic opportunity, rather than through military ties.

The outlines of a fairer and more just US Africa policy, in short, are not difficult to discern. Surely such a policy would be broadly welcomed in Africa – if not by Obiang, Mugabe, and their ilk. It would give new hope to Africa's people and show in no uncertain terms that the United States had become a positive force for change in the region, dedicated to a brighter African future.

The prospects for success, should a better Africa policy be adopted, will be affected by developments in Africa itself. The environment for deeper US engagement will be enhanced, for example, if Africa succeeds in its declared efforts to promote democracy, improve governance, and foster stability. The New Partnership for Africa's Development (NEPAD), an African Union program, is dedicated to strengthening the rule of law and promoting democratic political processes. The African Union itself, established in 2000, is a stronger organization than its predecessor, the Organization of African Unity, and has set the rejection of unconstitutional changes of government as one of its objectives. It has also given itself the right to intervene to prevent genocide and crimes against humanity. Within many African countries, meanwhile, there have been gains in democracy and in fighting corruption, although much remains to be done. If headway continues to be made in Africa toward greater democracy, improved governance, and political stability, US assistance in Africa can be more effective and prospects for trade and investment will improve. Setbacks will have the opposite effect.

But what changes would be required in the United States itself in order to bring about a new and better Africa policy? The list of obstacles is long and starts with the persistent reluctance of top US policymakers to see Africa as a policy priority. Pressing foreign policy problems related to Iraq, Iran, North Korea, and other countries distract the attention of policymakers and take away financial resources, which are tight in any case owing to the US budget deficit and the tax cuts granted wealthy Americans by the Bush administration and the Republican Congress. Nonetheless, incremental progress in Africa policy can be achieved in the near term. In November 2006, the American people elected a Congress with Democratic Party majorities in both houses. This Congress is likely to be more sympathetic than its predecessor to a fairer and more just Africa policy across a range of issues, from strengthening democracies and removing restrictions on AIDS programs to supporting the International Criminal Court. The odds of expanding spending for all types of AIDS prevention, including condom programs, and of removing the 'prostitution pledge' as well as the abstinence requirement from the PEPFAR legislation, are higher now, for example. The new Congress is expected to be far readier than the old to conduct oversight hearings and carry out investigations, and some of these may delve into administration conduct in Africa. The administration's policies toward Somalia and Equatorial Guinea could be sharply questioned, as could its response to the Darfur crisis and the deepening US military involvement in Africa. The decision to back Ethiopia's ouster of the Islamic Courts Union in Somalia, rather than looking for ways to contain the Union's expansionist impulses and engage in dialogue with moderate elements, may be a subject of particularly sharp debate. Congress will be constrained in the degree to which it can shift the US direction in Africa, however, because of the President's power to veto legislation, US budget problems, and the distractions of Middle East events. It is also a reality that many members, like policymakers in the executive branch, simply do not see Africa as a policy priority.

Further political change will take place in the United States in November 2008, when a new president is chosen, and it is possible to hope that this change will create another opportunity for the emergence of a better Africa policy. But the new president, like the Congress, will also be constrained by all of the underlying factors that have prevented policy change over the years. The key to overcoming these factors in the long term and shifting the direction of Africa policy lies in the development of a larger and more effective constituency for Africa able to insist upon and obtain policy change. This chapter presents evidence that this may now be happening. It will also argue that the growing numbers who favor a new approach to Africa must find new ways to enhance their influence, increase their numbers, and work together. Only then can Africa receive the attention it merits in US foreign policy.

Where might larger numbers of advocates for Africa be found? There are those in Washington who see increased interest in

Africa on the part of the Department of Defense and the broader defense community as a positive development because it is bringing in new voices in support of deeper US engagement with the region. There is something to be said for this view, even from the perspective of a fairer and more just Africa policy. The American defense community includes large numbers who are entirely pragmatic in their outlook and recognize that an overly large US military role in Africa could prove counterproductive. They also acknowledge that threats to US security interests in Africa can best be reduced over the long term through development rather than force.[2] Nonetheless, advocates for Africa should work to see to it that policymakers and Congress keep military influence over the making of Africa policy closely circumscribed. The 'long war' strategy that currently governs defense planning, with its concern for threats emerging from 'ungoverned spaces,' creates an ineluctable pressure for an expanded US military presence in Africa. So do the institutional pressures that lead the Defense Department as a whole, as well as units within the Department – such as EUCOM and CENTCOM, and the now-to-be-created Africa Command – to seek increased resources and greater responsibilities in the region. Policymakers should be vigilant to these pressures and resist them.

Advocates of deeper US engagement with Africa also sometimes look to the business community as a potential new source of support. The problem here is that, as noted in Chapter 2, US trade with Africa and US investment are just a tiny proportion of trade and investment worldwide. Consequently, the business community must inevitably be more concerned with US relations with other parts of the world than with Africa. American-owned oil companies in Africa do have a substantial financial stake in the region, and on theoretical grounds it might be argued that they have an interest in promoting improved governance and transparency. In practice, however, they are highly unlikely to become outspoken proponents of policies to advance these objectives because their bottom line often depends on maintaining good relations with authoritarian governments. Concerned about negative publicity arising from oil spills and other environmental damage, companies have sought to demonstrate their 'corporate responsibility' through community development programs and humanitarian initiatives, but little more can be expected of them.

New secular voices

While the defense and business communities are problematic as recruits to a wider constituency for Africa, there are important new voices in the secular world calling for a deeper US commitment to African development and relief. Some of these voices, as in the case of Bono, may have found their fundamental inspiration in a faith commitment, but they are principally addressing the secular world of public opinion and policymaking. Advocacy for Africa among the stars of music and entertainment has already been discussed, but strong support for a fairer and more just Africa policy is found elsewhere in the secular world as well.

Tremendous support is coming from two wealthy individuals whose fortunes were made not in Africa but elsewhere: Bill Gates of the Microsoft Corporation and investor Warren Buffett. Their engagement on African issues can only be applauded and it must be hoped that their spirit of generosity will serve as a model for others. The long-term impact of the Bill and Melinda Gates Foundation on African development and improved health will surely be immense. In 2006 alone, the Foundation announced more than $6 billion in health grants, most of which will benefit Africa directly or indirectly. These included a contribution of $24 million to the International AIDS Vaccine Initiative, a number of other major grants in support of vaccine development, and several grants to support the treatment and prevention of AIDS, tuberculosis, and malaria. In contrast to the US government, the Gates Foundation has been an enthusiastic backer of the Global Fund to Fight AIDS, Tuberculosis, and Malaria, stepping forward with $650 million in pledges to date – more than several major donor governments.[3] In September 2006, the Gates Foundation joined with the Rockefeller Foundation to launch the Alliance for a Green Revolution in Africa, initially funded at $150 million and focused on the development and distribution of high-yielding seeds. In June 2006, Buffett announced that he would begin turning over 85 per cent of his own vast fortune, valued at more than $40 billion, to the Gates Foundation, potentially doubling its assets. Buffett will join Bill and Melinda Gates on the Foundation's board.[4] Gates himself is gradually disengaging from Microsoft in order to devote himself full-time to the work of the Foundation. In addition to providing resources to Africa, the Bill and Melinda Gates team are major advocates for causes that benefit Africa. At the 2006 International AIDS Conference, held in Toronto, the two gave the keynote address and called for an expansion of prevention programs, an end to the strictures imposed by the US abstinence policy, and new efforts to deal with the stigma that inhibits efforts to slow the spread of HIV.

In July 2006, Bill and Melinda Gates joined up with another major advocate for Africa, former president Bill Clinton, to visit seven African nations, highlight the AIDS crisis, and call attention to the work the Gates Foundation and the Clinton Foundation are doing to fight it. The trip was widely reported and demonstrated the way in which new secular voices are raising Africa's profile on the global policy agenda.

President Clinton's Africa policies had certainly come in for their share of criticism when he was in office because of his administration's failed response to the Rwanda genocide, delays in dealing with the AIDS crisis, and other issues. In fairness, it should be said that after the Rwanda conflict, the Clinton administration gave new attention to the region, highlighted by the President's famous African tour in 1998, and found added resources for fighting AIDS. Moreover, as president, Clinton was limited in how much he could do for Africa by the 1994 election of a Republican Congress that was skeptical of foreign aid. In any event, since leaving office, Clinton's efforts on behalf of a better future for Africa have been impressive. Casting about for a post-presidential role, he attended the 2002 International AIDS Conference in Barcelona, where Nelson Mandela urged him to get involved in fighting AIDS in Africa and in helping bring down the cost of antiretrovirals.[5] Clinton answered the call, and working through the William J. Clinton Foundation, he was instrumental in achieving just what Mandela had asked of him. Negotiating with generic manufacturers and several donor countries, Clinton helped bring the cost of antiretroviral therapy in poor countries down from $500 to $120 per patient per year; and reduce the cost of testing patients for viral load during therapy as well. He gave a powerful speech of his own at the 2006 Toronto AIDS Conference, calling for increased global spending on AIDS and an expansion of prevention programs.[6] In contrast to the Gates Foundation, the Clinton Foundation has limited resources – its budget was just $30 million in 2006 – but it gives the former president the institutional backing he needs to bring his political skills and powers of persuasion to bear on the African AIDS epidemic and the other causes he has chosen to champion.[7]

US Senator Barack Obama, whose father was born in western Kenya, has the potential to emerge as another major voice in the constituency for Africa. The senator, a presidential candidate, drew wide coverage of his six-country trip to the region in August/September 2006, the highlight of which was a visit to his ancestral village and a conversation with his grandmother. At a camp for Darfur refugees in Chad, Obama called for the deployment of a UN force to Darfur and said US policy on the issue was 'better, but better is not good enough.'[8] Contributing by example to the struggle against the stigma of AIDS, Obama and his wife, Michelle, publicly took HIV blood tests at a mobile clinic in Kenya. 'If a United States Senator can get tested, anyone can get tested,' Obama said.[9] With the credibility granted by his African ancestry, the senator has more standing than most to address issues of transparency. He did not hesitate to do so, speaking out against corruption in Kenya and raising the issue in a meeting with President Mwai Kibaki.[10] In view of his duties as the representative of a very large American state, however, the senator may face limits on the time and attention he can devote to Africa. The realities of American politics may also impinge. Speaking on trade issues to journalists in Nairobi, Obama noted that he represented a strongly agricultural state and would try to reconcile the interests of farmers in Illinois with his desire that farmers in the developing world have access to American markets. But he concluded on a note favorable to Africa, saying, 'The US needs to open up its market to ensure that countries are not only recipients of aid but have the capacity to compete on world markets.'[11]

Other prominent Americans are active in causes that help Africa. For example, Richard Holbrooke, United Nations ambassador in the Clinton administration, is president and chief executive officer of the Global Business Council on HIV and AIDS. The Council works with member companies, including companies in Kenya, South Africa, and Botswana, to combat AIDS stigma among employees and encourage counseling and treatment in the workplace. Jeffrey Sachs, director of the Earth Institute at Columbia University, serves as Special Advisor to the UN secretary-general on the Millennium Development Goals and is tireless as an advocate of increased aid to end poverty and hunger in Africa. One wishes that there were more such advocates, but the point here is that there are now a number of prominent individuals in the secular world who are working for a better future for Africa, and they are strengthening the pro-Africa constituency in the United States.

Voices in the faith-based community

The Roman Catholic Church and the 'mainline' Protestant denominations in the United States, such as the Episcopal and Presbyterian churches, have long sponsored substantial outreach programs to Africa of their own, and supported US government efforts to promote development, human rights, and humanitarian relief. In recent years new voices in support of helping Africa have emerged and grown stronger in the large evangelical community as well. This development is raising the prospect of a broader and more effective constituency for Africa in the United States, but much work needs to be done to strengthen cooperation and coordination, not only between the evangelical and traditional churches, but also between the churches and advocates for Africa in the secular world.

The emergence of evangelicals as part of the constituency for Africa is an important development because the evangelical community is growing in numbers and influence. According to the Pew Forum on Religion and Public Life, more than 26 per cent of Americans now identify themselves as evangelical Protestants, while 17 per cent say they are Roman Catholic, and 16 per cent mainline Protestant.[12] The evangelical community has already made significant contributions to a fairer and more just Africa policy. US evangelicals joined with others in the faith-based community, for example, to push the July 2005 G8 summit for increased aid to Africa, debt cancellation, and justice in trade policy. American evangelicals were present among the demonstrators during the Gleneagles meeting, and Bob Geldof called them 'a huge force for change.'[13]

Liberal Christians and secularists may be wary of the prospect of working with evangelicals because they associate the movement with antiscientific attitudes, hostility to the United Nations, and a fixation on imminent apocalyptic 'end times.' These attitudes are certainly a concern with respect to the more fundamentalist wing of the evangelical movement. James Dobson, as noted in Chapter 3, has attacked the Global Fund, of all organizations, as a source of 'wickedness' in the world – underscoring the fact that little support for a fairer and more just Africa policy can be expected from that quarter. But according to the Pew Forum, more than half of evangelicals regard themselves as 'centrist' or 'modernist.' Fifty-eight per cent believe the United States should give a high priority to fighting AIDS, and 49 per cent would give a high priority for famine relief – not far below support levels among mainline Protestants, 63 per cent of whom favor giving AIDS priority and 53 per cent of whom want a priority for famine relief.[14] Among the unaffiliated, including secularists, 71 per cent would give priority to AIDS and 51 per cent to famine relief. Clearly there is a basis here for cooperation among a broad spectrum of Americans for a better Africa policy.

Rick Warren, founding pastor of Saddleback Church, a megacongregation in California, and author of a runaway bestseller, *The Purpose Driven Life*, has emerged as a particularly influential advocate for Africa. With other religious leaders, he has urged $2 billion in additional annual aid for Africa, and before Gleneagles he led a signature drive among church leaders on a letter to President Bush seeking 100 per cent debt forgiveness for poor countries, reform of trade rules, and an additional 1 per cent of the US budget for fighting AIDS, poverty, and hunger.[15] In contrast to Dobson, Warren has entered into a partnership with the Global Fund aimed at expanding the work of faith-based organizations in fighting AIDS. This partnership, announced in a joint appearance with Richard Feachem, Global Fund director at the 2006 Toronto AIDS conference, seems certain to boost support for the Fund among American churchgoers. Warren's PEACE plan for Africa seeks to 'plant new churches or partner with existing ones' – which is an area where Africa policymakers cannot and should not venture. But the plan also calls for assisting the poor, caring for the sick, and educating the next generation – all key elements of a fairer and more just Africa policy.

Within the evangelical movements, African-Americans are a particularly important source of support for Africa. Bishop Charles E. Blake, pastor of the West Angeles Church of God in Christ – which claims 24,000 congregants – is a frequent visitor to Africa and founder of the Pan African Children's Fund. The Fund has created the Save Africa's Children program, which provides support to more than 160 orphanages.[16] The Reverend Eugene Rivers of the Azusa Christian Community in Boston has founded the Pan African Charismatic Evangelical Congress, which aims 'to mobilize black church leadership globally to address the crisis in Africa and the African diaspora as it relates to the HIV/AIDS pandemic, the state of civil society, debt relief, and the spiritual conditions of the black poor.'[17] Bishop T. D. Jakes, a renowned Pentecostal preacher who enjoys a close relationship with President Bush – though he claims non-partisan status – was a co-signer of the Rick Warren letter sent to Bush before Gleneagles. Jakes' Faith to Africa: Kenya Mission is supporting a range of development projects in poor areas in that country.

A concern among some observers is that American evangelicals, in their commitment to mission and conversion, may exacerbate religious tensions and conflict in Africa, creating problems for US policymakers. While mission and conversion are basic to the evangelical vision, the fact is that the days when foreign missionaries were the driving force in evangelization in Africa are long past. Africa's burgeoning evangelical movement is African led, and its future in Africa – whatever direction it may take – is in African hands. American Christians may provide funds, books, and theological training within established denominations and through evangelical alliances, but the rise of Christianity in Africa is an African phenomenon independent of American support. Some African Christians, indeed, are now attempting to evangelize the United States.[18]

Perhaps the most interesting aspect of the American evangelical effort in Africa is that it is sending thousands of Americans to the region, including young people and active adults who go to Africa on brief mission trips. In this way, the evangelical movement is adding to the number of Americans who have not only lived among poor Africans, however briefly, but who also know African people on a personal basis. The only Americans with comparable experience are the thousands of returned Peace Corps volunteers. As the number of Americans with this sort of background grows, public support for a fairer and more just Africa policy will likely also increase.

Walter Russell Mead, Henry A. Kissinger senior fellow at the Council on Foreign Relations – a bastion of enlightened realist analysis of foreign policy – has argued that evangelical involvement in foreign affairs generally should be welcomed, not feared. In a 2006 article in the Council's influential journal, *Foreign Affairs*, Mead maintained that most evangelicals operate under a 'cheerier form of Calvinism' than fundamentalists, and that this often makes them 'open to, and even eager for, social action and cooperation with nonbelievers in projects to improve human welfare ... '[19] Mead noted that evangelicals 'are often suspicious of state-to-state aid and multilateral institutions,' and 'skeptical about grand designs and large-scale development efforts,'[20] but at the same time, they have thrown their weight behind PEPFAR, backed stronger US efforts on Darfur, and supported anti-human trafficking efforts. According to Mead, 'the rising evangelical establishment'[21] is gaining more and more experience in foreign affairs and becoming versed in its nuances and complexities. As this occurs, they will be able to persuade large numbers of Americans in the evangelical movement of the virtues of responsible engagement with the world.[22]

Despite Mead's optimism, the anti-Muslim views found among some evangelicals could prove problematic, should they become influential in Africa policy. Such views are not universal among evangelicals, although the Pew Forum has found that 46 per cent of white evangelical Protestants have an unfavorable opinion of Islam, while just 31 per cent have a favorable view. By contrast, 42 per cent of white mainline Protestants view Islam favorably as against 36 per cent with an unfavorable view. It is perhaps encouraging, however, that just 30 per cent of white evangelicals believe that the West is now engaged in a major conflict with Islam, just above the 28 per cent of mainline Protestants who hold this view. (Only 20 per cent of those with secular beliefs believe that a conflict with Islam is under way.)[23] Evangelical opinion is not yet pushing the United States into a war with Islam, but with evangelical leaders as prestigious as Franklin Graham calling Islam an evil religion after the 11 September 2001 attacks, and Pat Robertson insisting that the Koran teaches violence, there is reason for worry.[24] (Graham later said that he had meant to decry the violence done in the name of Islam, not the faith itself or Muslims generally.)[25] Should such views gain sway in the making of Africa policy, they could lead the United States in directions it ought not to go.

For Mead, such risks can be ameliorated if the broader foreign policy community engages with evangelical leaders in ongoing discussions of the great foreign policy issues of the day. To that end, the Council on Foreign Relations has launched an initiative on religion in public life, and is including in its discussions such figures as Rick Warren and Richard Land, president of the Southern Baptist Convention's Ethics and Religious Liberty Commission. The Pew Forum encourages similar discussions. Others should join these efforts to promote dialogue. It would be wise for the US-based African Studies Association, the major academic organization in the field, as well as think tanks and other organizations with an Africa focus, to promote exchanges with evangelicals focused on improving Africa policy. Evangelicals can bring to the table a strong voice in favor of helping the poor and promoting human rights – a voice that can contribute to bringing about a fairer and more just Africa policy.

Time for a China/US dialogue on Africa policy

The benefits of a fairer and more just US policy toward Africa could be vitiated unless the United States and China come to some agreement on the rules of conduct in the region. China is a surging economic and political influence in Africa, and if the United States should decide at some point to give Africa the priority it deserves, it could find that Chinese influence is an obstacle when it comes to promoting democracy, human rights, and transparency. China turns a blind eye to problems in these areas, and its policies have already hampered the limited US efforts to reduce the suffering in Darfur and improve conditions in Zimbabwe.

China's willingness to provide critically needed funds for infrastructure projects, including vital road and railway construction, as well as Chinese expertise and training, are welcomed in Africa and by all who support Africa's economic development. The seemingly insatiable Chinese demand for resources, including African resources, has boosted global commodity prices, contributing to the positive GDP growth seen in a number of African countries in recent years.

Chinese officials portray their country's indifference to the internal situations in African states as a virtue – one that sets them apart from the United States and the other Western donors. 'We respect the social system and development strategy pursued by African countries in light of their particular national conditions. We do not seek to export our own values and development models to Africa,' Premier Wen Jiabao told South African business leaders in June 2006.[26] As appealing as China's rhetoric may be to many African ears, however, it can translate into policies that are harmful to Africa's people. China fêted Zimbabwe's President Robert Mugabe in Beijing in July 2005, blunting Western criticism of the March 2005 parliamentary elections and the subsequent forced removal of 700,000 poor urban shantytown dwellers, suspected of supporting the opposition, in 'Operation Murambatsvina.' Even more disturbing are reports of Chinese military sales to the Mugabe regime. China's relations with Sudan, where it has a huge oil investment, are even closer than its ties to Zimbabwe and include a large arms component. In 2006, with the Darfur crisis raging, Amnesty International said that 'China has continued to allow military equipment to be sent to Sudan despite well-documented and widespread killings, rapes and abductions by government armed forces and allied military groups' in that region.[27]

Sudan and Zimbabwe are the most egregious examples of countries where China's policies run contrary to the interests of African people. But in other countries too China's willingness to extend aid and support on a 'no questions asked' basis is undermining efforts by African civil society organizations, international financial institutions, and Western donors to promote transparency and improvements in governance. Meanwhile, there is worry that the influx of cheap Chinese consumer goods, often sold in Chinese-owned shops, is harming indigenous entrepreneurs and traders, and that inexpensive Chinese textiles in African and global markets are driving Africa's nascent textile sector out of business.

Turning back China's growing involvement in Africa is neither possible nor desirable, but the United States ought to be leading a dialogue with China aimed at easing the harmful consequences of that involvement. China's investments in Africa mean that it has a long-term interest in peace and stability in the region.[28] By the same token, China's economic commitments in Africa are more likely to prosper in an environment of greater transparency and improved governance. Corrupt regimes and failing states are not going to be able to maintain Chinese-built infrastructure or repay loans. Moreover, China has an interest in nurturing Africa's own industries if the region is to become a genuine trading partner for China and not just a provider of raw materials.

Assistant Secretary Frazer visited China in November 2005, for conversations with Chinese officials at a comparable level of responsibility, as part of a broader State Department effort to promote China–US dialogue across a range of issues. On her return, Frazer said that 'I'm looking forward to continuing this dialogue. There are many areas where I think we absolutely can cooperate.'[29] Some meetings and consultations have taken place, but there is little evidence of substantive progress or of top-level involvement. President Bush and President Hu Jintao met at the White House in April 2006, and at the welcome ceremony Bush said that the two countries intended to deepen cooperation on several global issues, including 'the genocide in Darfur, Sudan.' But Bush made no further mention of Africa, and in his remarks in reply, President Hu was altogether silent on African topics.[30] Perhaps some progress has been made on Darfur. China did not, after all, veto the 31 August 2006 UN Security Council resolution authorizing a UN peacekeeping force for the region, and as noted in Chapter 5, it was given some credit in November 2006 reports – later called into question – suggesting that Khartoum had agreed to permit a joint UN–Africa peacekeeping force to deploy in Darfur. But it is not yet clear that China has been persuaded to put the sort of pressure on Khartoum that would be required to secure actual entry for the force.

With Bush administration officials so distracted by their Middle East policies, it will be up to the think tanks, the academic world, and advocacy groups to get a true dialogue under way, creating the basis for a more cooperative US–China relationship on African issues in the future. Initial efforts along these lines are being made at the Council on Foreign Relations and at the Center for Strategic and International Studies in Washington. Others concerned for a better future for Africa should be inviting Chinese representatives to Africa-related discussions and raising African issues in meetings with Chinese visitors or during trips to China. Through such efforts, these two powerful countries might ultimately find common ground on Africa policy and work together toward a better future for the continent.

Conclusion

While the elements of a fairer and more just US relationship with Africa are clear, the George W. Bush administration cannot be expected to lead the way toward the adoption of such a policy in its waning days. The distractions of the war the administration launched in Iraq, and of the other foreign policy as well as fiscal problems in which it is entangled, are simply too great to allow the current set of policymakers to give Africa the attention it deserves. Even should they want to do so, they would find that American capabilities have been reduced by the negative global public reaction to administration policies, and by the costs of the war in Iraq as well as the fiscal deficit.

The new Democratic Party-controlled Congress, however, has the opportunity to make incremental progress in some important areas, including AIDS policy and the quality of congressional oversight of the Administration's conduct in Africa. Further increases in aid to Africa will be delayed for a time, unfortunately, because the Republican-controlled Congress that left office at the end of 2006 failed to enact appropriations legislation to fund most government programs, including the foreign assistance program, in fiscal 2007. Democratic Party leaders in charge of the new Congress decided that most spending for 2007 would simply be continued at 2006 levels because consideration of the un-passed appropriations bills would detract from their ability to move forward on other priorities, including a change in course in Iraq.

A better day for Africa in US foreign policy is probably going to have to await a new administration and one that is no longer burdened by the Iraq commitment. Such an administration will likely want to restore the reputation of the United States as a country with strong commitments to peace, democracy, human rights, and development – and Africa would be a good place to make a start. In the meantime, those who seek a better Africa policy have a responsibility to work together to raise public consciousness of Africa's needs and to find consensus on the best means of responding. A strong foundation is already being laid by Africa's traditional supporters and by influential new advocates in both the secular and faith-based worlds. Dialogue and coordination are essential among these advocates for Africa if progress is to be made – even though secular advocates, representatives of the mainline Christian denominations, and evangelicals are not very used to conversation with one another. There must also be a dialogue with China on a better future for Africa. Through such efforts and initiatives, a fairer and more just Africa policy can be made ready for implementation when the United States finally emerges from the foreign policy and fiscal difficulties in which the Bush administration has placed it.

Notes

1 Introduction

1 In American parlance, the term 'administration' refers to that part of the executive branch consisting of the President and his political appointees. These encompass all members of the cabinet, such as the Secretary of State and the Secretary of Defense, and their top-level assistants, including the Assistant Secretary of State for African Affairs. The National Security Council at the White House and its Senior Director for African Affairs are also part of 'the administration.' Congress, the career civil service, and the professional military are not.

2 White House, 'Africa policy,' available at <www.whitehouse.gov/infocus/africa/>.

3 Warren S. Howard, *American Slavers and the Federal Law, 1837–1862* (Berkeley: University of California Press, 1963; reprinted by Greenwood Press, 1976), p. 60.

4 Raymond W. Copson, *Executive-Legislative Consultation on Foreign Policy: Sanctions Against Rhodesia* (Washington, DC: US Government Printing Office, 1982).

5 Public Law (P.L.) 99-8, the African Famine Relief and Recovery Act of 1985, authorized this assistance, while an emergency supplemental appropriation, P.L. 99-10, provided $784 million in funding. See Carol Lancaster, 'The 99th Congress and the African economic crisis,' in US Congress, House Committee on Foreign Affairs, *Congress and Foreign Policy, 1985–1986*, Committee Print (Washington, DC: US Government Printing Office, 1988), p. 147.

6 P.L. 99-440, the Comprehensive Anti-Apartheid Act of 1986. See Robert B. Shepard, 'The 99th Congress and South Africa sanctions,' in ibid., pp. 13–26.

7 Hans J. Morgenthau, *Politics among Nations: The Struggle for Power and Peace*, 5th edn (New York: Alfred A. Knopf, 1973), p. 5.

8 US Congress, Senate, Select Committee to Study Governmental Operations with Respect to Intelligence Activities ('Church Committee'), *Alleged Assassination Plots Involving Foreign Leaders: An Interim Report*, Senate Report no. 94-465 (Washington, DC: US Government Printing Office, 1975), pp. 13–70.

9 Second Gore–Bush presidential debate, 11 October 2000. Available at <www.debates.org>.

10 See, for example, Zbigniew Brzezinski, 'If we must fight … ,' *Washington Post*, 18 August 2002; or Jeffrey Goldberg, 'Letter from Washington, breaking ranks: what turned Brent Scowcroft against the Bush administration?,' *New Yorker*, 31 October 2005. Scowcroft was National Security Advisor to the first President Bush.

11 A presidential initiative to end hunger in Africa was announced by Secretary of State Powell at the 2002 World Summit on Sustainable Development in Johannesburg. White House, 'Fact sheet: the advance of freedom and hope,' 22 May 2003.

12 John G. Fox, 'Approaching humanitarian intervention strategically: the case of Somalia,' *SAIS Review* 21 (Winter–Spring 2001), pp. 147–58.

13 UN Security Council Resolution 794, 3 December 2002.

14 Kevin Phillips, *American Theocracy: The Peril and Politics of Radical Religion, Oil, and Borrowed Money in the 21st Century* (New York: Viking, 2006), p. 81; F. William Engdahl, 'Speaking freely: the oil factor in Bush's "War on Tyranny",' *Asia Times Online*, 3 May 2005 <www.atimes.com>; Mark Fineman, 'The Oil Factor in Somalia,' *Los Angeles Times*, 18 January 1993.

15 The Refugee Policy Group estimated that 10,000 lives were saved after the US intervention, while 100,000–125,000 were lost owing to earlier delays in decisive international action. The total death toll was estimated at 202,000–238,000. Refugee Policy Group, *Lives Lost, Lives Saved: Excess Mortality and the Impact of Health Interventions in the Somalia Emergency*, prepared under a contract with the US Office of Foreign Disaster Assistance (Washington, DC: 1994).

16 Stephen Mansfield, *The Faith of George W. Bush* (Lake Mary, FL: Charisma House, 2003), p. 109; Paul Kengor, *God and George W. Bush: A Spiritual Life* (New York: HarperCollins, Regan Books, 2004), p. 61.

17 Jeffrey Goldberg, 'Letter from Washington, the believer: George W. Bush's loyal speechwriter,' *New Yorker* (13 and 20 February 2006).

18 In his 31 January 2006 State of the Union Address, the President said that the United States could not retreat in the face of 'radical Islam' and would never 'surrender to evil.' On 10 August 2006, following the UK arrests of suspects in a plot to bomb airliners, the President said, 'this nation is at war with Islamic fascists.' Available at <www.whitehouse.gov>.

19 'Liberia: Ellen Johnson-Sirleaf on Oprah's Wednesday broadcast, continues push for investment and rebuilding assistance,' <allAfrica.com>, 16 May 2006.

20 Biography of Edward W. Scott, Jr, at the website of the Center for Global Development, <www.cgdev.org>.

21 'Priorities,' <www.congressionalblackcaucus.net>.

22 US Department of Justice, *Report of the Attorney General to the Congress of the United States on the Administration of the Foreign Agents Registration Act of 1938, as Amended for the Six Months Ending June 30, 2004*, Washington, DC. Available at <www.usdoj.gov>.

2 Aid, trade, and development

1 World Bank, *World Development Indicators, 2006* (Washington, DC: 2006), Table 2.7.

2 Ibid.

3 World Bank, *African Development Indicators, 2006* (Washington, DC: 2006), Table 2.21.

4 For a list of the MDGs, see <www.un.org>, click on 'UN Millennium Development Goals.'

5 White House, 'President discusses G8 summit, progress in Africa,' 30 June 2005.

6 White House, 'President addresses United Nations high-level plenary meeting,' 14 September 2005.

7 White House, 'Fighting malaria in Africa,' press release, 30 June 2005.

8 For coverage of possible assistance policy reforms in this area, visit the website of the Partnership to Cut Hunger and Poverty in Africa, <www.africanhunger.org>.

9 Susan E. Rice, using somewhat different data, figures the Bush increase at 67 per cent. 'US foreign assistance to Africa: claims vs. reality' (Washington, DC: Brookings Institution, 27 June 2005). Rice, who served as Assistant Secretary of State for African Affairs in the Clinton administration, also noted that the Bush Administration's increase over the Clinton years was less than claimed when inflation was taken into account. The Republican Congresses faced by President Clinton from 1994 were also partly responsible for aid levels in the Clinton years. Nicholas D. Kristof, 'Aid: can it work,' *New York Review of Books*, 5 October 2006.

10 This was pointed out to the author by Larry Nowels, then serving as a specialist in foreign assistance at the Congressional Research Service.

11 Final funding levels for 2007 remained uncertain at the time of writing, since the Republican-controlled Congress that left office at the end of 2006 did not complete action on foreign assistance appropriations. It seemed likely that the new Democratic Congress, as a temporary measure, would fund most programs at levels close to 2006 spending, while funding international AIDS programs at or above requested levels. The upward trend in aid to Africa was thought likely to resume in fiscal 2008.

12 Charles E. Hanrahan, *Agricultural Export and Food Aid Programs* (Washington, DC: Congressional Research Service Issue Brief IB98006, 6 March 2006), available at <www.opencrs.com>.

13 Public Law 109-234, Title I.

14 'Promises? What promises?' *New York Times* editorial, 22 May 2006.

15 Nicholas D. Kristof, *New York Times*, 5 July 2005.

16 Organization for Economic Cooperation and Development, 'Statistical annex of the 2005 Development Co-operation Report,' Table 29, available at <www.oecd.org>.

17 Ibid.

18 Council on Foreign Relations, *More than Humanitarianism: A Strategic US Approach Toward Africa* (New York: January 2006), p. 117.

19 Peter Timmer, 'Global Development: Views from the Center, the Politics of Food Aid' (Center for

Global Development: 2 November 2005), available at <www.cgdev.org>.

20 Lawrence MacDonald, 'Global development: views from the center, Natsios vows to pursue food aid reform,' Center for Global Development, 9 December 2005; Celia W. Dugger, 'Saturday profile: planning to fight poverty from outside the system,' *New York Times*, 14 January 2006.

21 Carol Lancaster and Ann Van Dusen, *Organizing US Foreign Aid: Confronting Challenges of the Twenty-first Century* (Washington, DC: Brookings Institution, 2005), p. 11.

22 Larry Nowels, *Millennium Challenge Account: Implementation of a New US Foreign Aid Initiative* (Washington, DC: Congressional Research Service Report RL32427, 7 February 2006), available at <www.opencrs.com>.

23 White House, 'President proposes $5 billion plan to help developing nations: remarks by the president on global development, Inter-American Development Bank,' 14 March 2002.

24 USAID, *Policy Framework for Bilateral Foreign Aid* (Washington, DC: January 2006), p. 1.

25 USAID, *Budget Justification to the Congress, Fiscal Year 2006, Africa* (Washington, DC: 2005).

26 Nicholas van de Walle, *African Economies and the Politics of Permanent Crisis, 1979–1999* (Cambridge: Cambridge University Press, 2001), pp. 275–6.

27 USAID, *Budget Justification to the Congress.*

28 Council on Foreign Relations, *More than Humanitarianism*, p. 125.

29 William Easterly, *The White Man's Burden: Why the West's Efforts to Aid the Rest Have Done So Much Ill and So Little Good* (New York: Penguin Press, 2006), pp. 368–9.

30 Ibid., p. 50. For a review of the foreign assistance debate, see Nicholas D. Kristof, 'Aid: can it Work,' *New York Review of Books*, 5 October 2006.

31 See <www.thehelpcommission.gov>.

32 Lancaster and Van Dusen, *Organizing US Foreign Aid*, pp. 57–8.

33 White House, 'President Bush signs African Growth and Opportunity Act: remarks by the President at signing of the AGOA Acceleration Act of 2004,' 13 July 2004.

34 Calculated on the basis of data appearing in US Office of International Trade Administration, *Foreign Trade Highlights*, Tables 6 and 7, appearing at <http://ita.doc.gov>.

35 Calculated on the basis of data appearing in US Department of Commerce, Bureau of Economic Analysis, 'US direct investment abroad: country detail for selected items,' available at <www.bea.gov>.

36 Council on Foreign Relations, *More than Humanitarianism*, p. 123.

37 Trade and Development Act of 2000, Public Law 106-200, Title 1.

38 AGOA Acceleration Act of 2004, Public Law 108-274.

39 Available at <www.agoa.gov>,

click on '4th AGOA Forum' and 'Highlighted AGOA Success Stories.'

40 'US–African trade profile,' March 2006, available at <www.agoa.gov>.

41 Office of the United States Trade Representative, *African Growth and Opportunity Act Competitiveness Report* (Washington, DC: July 2005), pp. 2–3. See also, Corporate Council on Africa, 'AGOA: a five year assessment,' testimony of Stephen Hayes, president, before the House Committee on International Relations, Subcommittee on Africa, Global Human Rights, and International Operations, 20 October 2005.

42 OECD, *Agricultural Policies in OECD Countries: Monitoring and Evaluation, 2005, Highlights*, p. 75, available at <www.oecd.org>.

43 Oxfam, *Finding the Moral Fiber: Why Reform Is Urgently Needed for a Fair Cotton Trade* (18 October 2004).

44 Randy Schnepf, *US Agricultural Policy Response to WTO Cotton Decision* (Washington, DC: Congressional Research Service Report RS22187, 31 March 2006), p. 6, available at <www.opencrs.com>.

45 These speeches are cited above.

46 Larry Rohter, 'Agriculture discord stymies world trade talks' revival,' *New York Times*, 11 September 2006.

47 See, for example, Chantelle Benjamin, 'US, SACU to meet to revive flagging free-trade talks,' *Business Day* (Johannesburg), 18 April 2006; Wezi Tjaronda, 'SACU and USA bog down on trade,' *New Era* (Windhoek), 20 April 2006; Danielle Langton, *United States-Southern African Customs Union (SACU) Free Trade Agreement Negotiations: Background and Potential Issues* (Washington, DC: Congressional Research Service Report RS21387, 3 January 2005), available at <www.opencrs.com>.

48 Todd Moss, 'Briefing: the G8's multilateral debt relief intiative and poverty reduction in sub-Saharan Africa,' *African Affairs* 105 (April 2006), pp. 285–93.

49 Raymond W. Copson, *Africa, the G8, and the Blair Initiative* (Washington, DC: Congressional Research Service Report RL32796, 20 July 3005).

50 Moss, 'Briefing,' p. 291.

3 AIDS policy

1 UNAIDS, *AIDS Epidemic Update, December 2000* (Geneva: 2000), p. 10.

2 UNAIDS, *Report on the Global AIDS Epidemic, June 2000* (Geneva: 2000), pp. 8–9.

3 John Donnelly, 'Prevention urged in AIDS fight: Natsios says fund should spend less on HIV treatment,' *Boston Globe*, 7 June 2001.

4 Greg Behrman, *The Invisible People: How the US Has Slept Through the Global AIDS Pandemic, the Greatest Humanitarian Catastrophe of Our Time* (New York: Free Press, 2004), p. 257.

5 Helms's conversion was limited to AIDS in Africa, and he refused to alter his views on domestic AIDS

issues involving homosexuals. 'Sen. Helms clarifies AIDS comments,' Associated Press, 6 March 2002.

6 Behrman, *The Invisible People*, pp. 273–7; James Traub, 'The statesman,' *New York Times Magazine*, 18 September 2005; Ron Suskind, *The Price of Loyalty: George W. Bush, the White House, and the Education of Paul O'Neill* (New York: Simon and Schuster, 2004), pp. 250–59.

7 Behrman, *The Invisible People*, p. 270; Traub, 'The Statesman.'

8 Behrman, *The Invisible People*, pp. 273, 275.

9 US Congress, Senate, *United States Leadership Against HIV/AIDS, Tuberculosis, and Malaria Act of 2002*, Report to Accompany S. 2525, Senate Report 107-206 (Washington, DC: US Government Printing Office, 3 July 2002).

10 Carl M. Cannon, 'Soul of a conservative,' *National Journal*, 13 May 2005; Jeffrey Goldberg, 'Letter from Washington: the believer: George W. Bush's loyal speechwriter,' *New Yorker*, 13 and 20 February 2006, p. 57.

11 White House, 'President Bush discusses plan for emergency AIDS relief in Uganda,' 11 July 2003; also cited in Behrman, *The Invisible People*, p. 308.

12 Behrman, *The Invisible People*, pp. 301–2.

13 Michiko Kakutani, 'Critic's notebook: all the President's books,' *New York Times*, 11 May 2006. This article reviews a number of books on the Bush administration.

14 Behrman, *The Invisible People*, p. 202.

15 For more on the internal administration deliberations, see Berman, *The Invisible People*, pp. 288–95.

16 Nicolas Cook, *AIDS in Africa* (Washington, DC: Congressional Research Service Issue Brief IB10050, 9 March 2006), as well as earlier versions by Raymond W. Copson. These totals include spending through the State Department's GHAI, as well as through USAID's Child Survival and Health program and the Centers for Disease Control and Prevention of the Department of Health and Human Services.

17 'Politics and policy: US official defends policy on generic AIDS Drugs; business coalition says policy undermining efforts to fight disease,' Henry J. Kaiser Family Foundation, *Daily HIV/AIDS Report*, 1 April 2004.

18 UNAIDS, *Report on the Global AIDS Epidemic, June 2004* (Geneva: 2004), p. 191.

19 Speech to the Third International AIDS Society Conference, 24 July 2005.

20 Based on information available at the Global Fund website, <www.theglobalfund.org>.

21 Raymond W. Copson and Tiaji Salaam, *The Global Fund to Fight AIDS, Tuberculosis, and Malaria: Background and Current Issues* (Washington, DC: Congressional Research Service Report RL31712, 3 June 2005).

22 Behrman, *The Invisible People*, p. 260.

23 John Donnelly, 'Briton to head Global Fund on diseases post

seen critical in allotting assets to combat AIDS,' *Boston Globe*, 25 April 2002. The administration had reportedly favored George Moose, an Assistant Secretary of State for Africa in the Clinton administration.

24 J. Stephen Morrison and Todd Summers, 'United to fight HIV/AIDS?,' *Washington Quarterly*, Autumn 2003, p. 183.

25 *Global Fund Observer*, 8 November 2004. Available at <www.aidspan.org>.

26 Ibid. See also Copson and Salaam, *The Global Fund.*

27 Office of the Global AIDS Coordinator, *Emergency Plan for AIDS Relief Fiscal Year 2005 Operational Plan, June 2005 Update*, p. 168.

28 Daniel Burke, 'Rift opens among evangelicals on AIDS funding,' Religion News Service, 1 June 2006.

29 Ibid.

30 Friends of the Global Fight Against AIDS, Tuberculosis, and Malaria, 'Fact sheet: a response to misperceptions surrounding the global fund to fight AIDS, Tuberculosis, and Malaria,' Washington, DC, June 2006.

31 Global Fund, 'The Global Fund's first replenishment, 2006–2007, chair's report,' 16 September 2005.

32 These provisions are found in Sec. 202 of P.L. 108-25, The United States Leadership against HIV/AIDS, Tuberculosis, and Malaria Act of 2003, as amended by P.L. 108-199, the FY2004 Consolidated Appropriations.

33 Jennifer Kates, *Financing the Response to HIV/AIDS in Low and Middle Income Countries: Funding for HIV/AIDS from the G7 and European Commission* (Washington, DC: Kaiser Family Foundation, July 2005), p. 10.

34 UNAIDS, *Resource Needs for an Expanded Response to AIDS in Low and Middle Income Countries*, August 2005. The funds likely to be provided in 2006 include $2.8 billion expected from the afflicted countries themselves.

35 See <www.whitehouse.gov/infocus/hivaids/>.

36 Amy Belasco, *The Cost of Iraq, Afghanistan, and Other Global War on Terrorism Operations Since 9/11* (Washington, DC: Congressional Research Service Report RL33110, 22 September 2006). Belasco calculates total appropriations for the Global War on Terror at $437 billion.

37 'UN Special Envoy Stephen Lewis and US Congresswoman Barbara Lee decry gaps in US global AIDS policy; propose a way forward,' *USA Newswire*, 14 August 2006.

38 Under the law, the 33 per cent provision was in the form of a recommendation in 2004 and 2005, but mandatory for 2006 through 2008.

39 'Congressman Joe Pitts' biography pages,' available at <www.house.gov>.

40 US Government Accountability Office (GAO), *Global Health: Spending Requirement Presents Challenges for Allocating Prevention Funding under the President's Emer-*

gency Plan for AIDS Relief (Washington, DC: GAO Report GAO-06-395, April 2006), p. 21.

41 Ibid., p. 5.

42 Stephen Collinson, 'US blasts AIDS plan critics,' AFP, 16 August 2006.

43 GAO, *Global Health*, pp. 15–16.

44 Ibid., pp. 27–8.

45 US Department of State, Office of the Global AIDS Coordinator, *Action Today, a Foundation for Tomorrow: The President's Emergency Plan for AIDS Relief, Second Annual Report to Congress* (Washington, DC: 2006), p. 26.

46 'Making money work for people on the ground,' Speech at the opening ceremony of ICASA (International Conference on HIV/AIDS and Sexually Transmitted Infections in Africa) 2005 (Abuja, Nigeria: 4 December 2005).

47 Human Rights Watch, *The Less They Know the Better: Abstinence-Only HIV/AIDS Programs in Uganda* (March 2005). Available at <www.hrw.org>.

48 Katy Pownall, 'Ugandans report mixed message on AIDS plan,' Associated Press, 18 March 2006.

49 'Kenya's First Lady decries use of condoms,' Reuters, 19 May 2006.

50 See the sub-Saharan Africa discussion in UNAIDS, *AIDS Epidemic Update: December 2005*; also Celia W. Dugger, 'Where AIDS galloped, lessons in applying the reins,' *New York Times*, 18 May 2006.

51 Daniel T. Halperin et al., 'The time has come for common ground on preventing sexual transmission of HIV,' *The Lancet* 364 (27 November 2004): 1913–15.

52 Rita Beamish, 'Religious groups get chunk of AIDS money,' Associated Press, 30 January 2006.

53 'President discusses G8 Summit, progress in Africa,' 30 June 2005. Available at <www.whitehouse.gov>.

54 'White House changes tune on AIDS groups working overseas,' *USA Today*, 9 June 2005.

55 'US anti-prostitution gag for AIDS work unconstitutional, rules US Judge,' *AIDSMAP News*, 12 May 2006; Glenn Kessler, 'Prostitution clause in AIDS policy ruled illegal,' *Washington Post*, 19 May 2006.

56 UNAIDS, *Uniting the World against AIDS: 2006 Report on the Global AIDS Epidemic* (Geneva: June 2006), p. 15.

57 World Health Organization and UNAIDS, 'Fact sheet: progress in scaling up access to HIV treatment in low and middle-income countries, June 2006,' 16 August 2006.

58 UNAIDS and World Health Organization, 'Fact sheet 06: sub-Saharan Africa.'

59 Stephen Smith, 'Study finds AIDS effort helps economies,' *Boston Globe*, 18 August 2006.

60 Office of the Global AIDS Coordinator, *Action Today*.

61 Lawrence K. Altman, 'AIDS Effort in Zambia hailed as a success,' *New York Times*, 14 August 2006.

4 Democracy and human rights

1 For an insightful review of these and other key characteristics of African politics, see Goran Hyden, *African Politics in Comparative Perspective* (Cambridge: Cambridge University Press, 2006).

2 Michael Bratton and Wonbin Cho, compilers, *Where Is Africa Going: Views from Below*, Working Paper no. 60: May 2006), p. 17. Data are for 'circa 2005.' The compilers noted some drop in support for democracy, owing to concerns over corruption and disappointment with the conduct of elected leaders in some countries.

3 Two recent books explore these themes with respect to the nineteenth century: Sean Wilentz. *The Rise of American Democracy: Jefferson to Lincoln* (New York: Norton, 2005); Garry Wills, *'Negro President': Jefferson and the Slave Power* (New York: Houghton Mifflin, 2003).

4 US Department of State, 'Remarks by Condoleezza Rice, US Secretary of State: new direction for US foreign assistance,' Washington, DC: 19 January 2006.

5 US Department of State, 'Remarks at the Southern Baptist Convention Annual Convention,' 14 June 2006.

6 Remarks at a meeting on transformational development convened by the Center for Global Development, Washington, DC: 20 January 2006.

7 Testimony before the Senate Foreign Relations Committee, 18 January 2005. The others were Cuba, Burma, Iran, North Korea, and Belarus.

8 'Freeing a nation from a tyrant's grip,' *New York Times*, 24 June 2003.

9 White House, 'President Bush meets with South African President Mbeki, press availability with President Bush and President Mbeki of South Africa,' 9 July 2003.

10 International Crisis Group, *Post Election Zimbabwe, What Next*, Africa Report no. 93 (Pretoria/Brussels: 7 June 2005), p. 21.

11 International Crisis Group, *Zimbabwe's Continuing Self-Destruction*, Africa Briefing No. 38 (Pretoria/Brussels: 6 June 2006), p. 19.

12 The administration's general reluctance to appoint special envoys is discussed in Chapter 5.

13 On these issues, see Gideon Maltz, 'Zimbabwe policy: preparing for the post-Mugabe era,' Center for Strategic and International Studies, *Online Africa Policy Forum*, 10 November 2006. Available at <http://forums.csis.org/africa/>.

14 Letter dated 27 April 2006.

15 Ken Silverstein, 'Our friend Teodoro: Equatorial Guinea's leader visits the Beltway,' *Harper's Magazine Blog* <www.harpers.org>, 18 April 2006. The proclamation was issued on 12 January 2004.

16 US Department of Energy, Energy Information Administration, 'Country analysis briefs: Equatorial Guinea,' updated May 2006. Available at <www.eia.doe.gov>.

17 USAID, 'USAID and the Republic of Equatorial Guinea agree

to unique partnership for development: Tobias calls memorandum of understanding "landmark agreement,"' Press release, 11 April 2006.

18 World Bank, Equatorial Guinea 'Country Brief,' available at <www.worldbank.org>.

19 US Department of State, *Country Reports on Human Rights Practices 2005* (Washington, DC: March 2006). These reports are required by Congress.

20 Letter from Senator Biden to President Bush dated 19 May 2006.

21 National Defense Authorization for Fiscal Year 2006, Public Law 109-163.

22 US Naval Forces Europe, 6th Fleet Public Affairs, 'Framework for action plan adopted at ministerial conference,' 15 November 2006. Available at <www.eucom.mil>.

23 US Department of State, *Country Reports on Human Rights Practice, 2005* (Washington, DC: March 2006).

24 <www.whitehouse.gov>, search on 'Omar Bongo.'

25 Phil Shenon, 'Lobbyist sought $9 million to set Bush meeting,' *New York Times*, 10 November 2005.

26 Jennifer Elsea, *US Policy Regarding the International Criminal Court* (Washington, DC: Congressional Research Service Report RL31495, 26 April 2006), p. 3.

27 United States Mission to the United Nations, 'Explanation of position by Eric Rosand, Legal Advisor, on the adoption of resolution concerning the report of the International Criminal Court, in the Sixth Committee, 19 November 2004,' Press release (New York: 19 November 2004).

28 Elsea, *US Policy*, p. 1.

29 Whether these agreements should properly be called 'Article 98' agreements is doubtful. See Elsea, *US Policy*, footnotes 52 and 53.

30 Coalition for the International Criminal Court, 'Summary of information on Bilateral Immunity Agreements (BIAs) of so-called "Article 98 Agreements" as of July 8, 2006,' available at <www.iccnow.org>.

31 Mark Mazzetti, 'US cuts in Africa aid hurt war on terror and increase China's influence, officials say,' *New York Times*, 23 July 2006.

32 The waiver covered twenty-two countries worldwide, including the six African countries that had refused to sign Article 98 agreements.

33 <www.usaid.gov>. Click on 'Our work.'

34 <www.ned.org>. Click on 'About.'

35 Barbara Conry, 'Loose cannon: the National Endowment for Democracy' (Washington, DC: Cato Institute, 1993).

36 Tom Barry, 'The NED's latest front group: inside Bush's World Movement for Democracy' (*Counterpunch*, 4 August 2005), available at <www.counterpunch.org>.

37 Bart Jones, 'US funds aid Chavez opposition,' *National Catholic Reporter* (2 April 2004); 'US Gvt. channels millions through National Endowment for Democracy to fund

anti-Lavalas groups in Haiti,' *Democracy Now!* (23 January 2006), available at <www.democracynow.org>.

38 Calculated on the basis of data appearing in NED annual reports.

39 Quoted in Thomas Carothers, 'The backlash against democracy promotion,' *Foreign Affairs* 85 (March/April 2006), p. 58.

40 'Nigeria: death of 3rd term, victory for democracy – US,' *This Day* (Lagos), 31 May 2006.

41 US Department of State, 'Ethiopia: US envoy Yamamoto continues personal diplomacy,' 31 May 2006.

42 Terrence Lyons, 'Ethiopia in 2005: the beginning of the transition?', Center for Strategic and International Studies Africa Notes (January 2006).

43 'Answering the challenges of lofty rhetoric,' *Washington Post*, 19 June 2006.

5 Conflict and peacekeeping

1 'President discusses peace agreement in Sudan,' White House press release, 8 May 2006.

2 <www.savedarfur.org>, click on 'Situation in Darfur.' A study reported in a scientific journal estimated the death toll at 255,000, although the authors believed the figure could be as high as 400,000. John Hagan and Alberto Palloni, 'Death in Darfur,' *Science* 313 (15 September 2006): 1578–9; Jeffrey Gettleman, 'Toll of Darfur underreported, study declares,' *New York Times*, 15 September 2006.

3 US Agency for International Development, 'Sudan complex emergency situation report #5, fiscal year 2007,' 1 December 2006.

4 US Committee for Refugees and Immigrants, *World Refugee Survey 2006*, Table 9.

5 Benjamin Coghlan et al., 'Mortality in the Democratic Republic of Congo: a nationwide survey,' *Lancet* 367 (7 January 2006): 44–51.

6 Mark Mazzetti, 'Efforts by CIA fail in Somalia, officials charge,' *New York Times*, 8 June 2006.

7 Mark Lacey, 'Somali Islamists declare victory: warlords on run,' *New York Times*, 6 June 2006.

8 White House, 'Danforth to lead search for peace as special envoy,' Press release, 6 September 2001.

9 Mark Lacey, 'Death of Sudan rebel leader imperils fragile hope for peace,' *New York Times*, 2 August 2005.

10 John C. Danforth, 'Onward, moderate Christian soldiers,' *New York Times*, 17 June 2005.

11 US Department of State, Office of the Spokesman, 'Fact sheet: chronology of US engagement in the Sudan peace process,' 8 January 2005.

12 Emergency Supplemental Appropriations Act for Defense, the Global War on Terror, and Hurricane Recovery, 2006, Public Law 109-234, signed into law 15 June 2006.

13 Save Darfur Coalition, 'Coalition applauds President's call for UN peacekeepers and appointment of Andrew Natsios as special envoy,' Press release, 19 September 2006.

14 Michael Fullilove, 'All the President's men,' *Foreign Affairs* 84 (March/April 2005).

15 Glenn Kessler, 'US envoy joins negotiations on Darfur as deadline is extended,' *Washington Post*, 3 May 2006.

16 Julie Flint, 'Dealing with the Devil in Darfur,' *New York Times*, 17 June 2006. For background and analysis on the Darfur crisis, see Julie Flint and Alex de Waal, *Darfur: A Short History of a Long War*, African Arguments Series (London: Zed Books in association with the International African Institute, 2005).

17 Helene Cooper, 'No. 2 State Department official resigns to join Wall Street firm,' *New York Times*, 20 June 2006.

18 Secretary Colin L. Powell, 'The crisis in Darfur,' Testimony presented on 9 September 2004.

19 H.Con.Res. 467 and S.Con. Res. 133, both adopted on 22 July 2004.

20 Jim VandeHei, 'In break with UN, Bush calls Sudan killings genocide,' *Washington Post*, 2 June 2005.

21 *Report of the International Commission of Inquiry on Darfur to the United Nations Secretary-General Pursuant to Security Council Resolution 1564 of 18 September 2004* (Geneva: 25 January 2005), p. 73.

22 International Criminal Court, *Third Report of the Prosecutor of the International Criminal Court to the UN Security Council Pursuant to UNSCR 1593* (Geneva: 14 June 2006), p. 1.

23 Public Law 109-234, cited above. This legislation also provided new funds to GPOI to make up for the amount reprogrammed earlier for the African Mission in Sudan (AMIS).

24 Victoria K. Holt, 'Testimony, Hearing on African Organizations and Institutions: positive cross-continental progress,' presented before the Subcommittee on African Affairs, Senate Foreign Relations Committee (Washington, DC: Henry L. Stimson Center, 17 November 2005), pp. 7–9.

25 Marjorie Browne, *United Nations Peacekeeping: Issues for Congress* (Washington, DC: Congressional Research Service Issue Brief IB90103, 5 July 2005).

26 Council on Foreign Relations, *More than Humanitarianism: A Strategic US Approach toward Africa* (New York: January 2006), p. 86.

27 Alex de Waal, 'Darfur: time for diplomacy, not confrontation,' Center for Strategic and International Studies, Online Africa Policy Forum, 22 September 2006. Available at <http://forums.csis.org/africa/>.

28 Human Rights Watch, *World Report 2005*, available at <www.hrw.org>.

29 White House, 'President's statement on violence in Darfur, Sudan,' 9 September 2004.

30 White House, 'President welcomes NATO Secretary General to the White House,' 20 March 2006.

31 White House, 'President discusses peace agreement in Sudan,' 8 May 2006.

32 UN Security Council 1706 (2006).

33 National Public Radio, 'United Nations weighs sanctions for Sudan officials,' 27 February 2006.

34 'A US plan for Darfur,' *Boston Globe*, 10 April 2006.

35 Susan E. Rice, Anthony Lake, and Donald M. Payne, 'We saved Europeans. Why not Africans?,' *Washington Post*, 2 October 2006.

36 De Waal, 'Darfur.'

37 J. Stephen Morrison and Chester A. Crocker, 'Time to focus on the real choices in Darfur,' *Washington Post*, online *Think Tank Town*, 7 November 2006.

38 Nicholas D. Kristof, 'If not now, when?,' *New York Times*, 29 October 2006.

39 Thirty per cent would prefer intervention by a UN force and 22 per cent intervention by an African Union force in a 'conflict like Darfur.' Only 5 per cent would support intervention by a rich country. Program on International Policy Attitudes (PIPA), Globescan, and Knowledge Networks, *The Darfur Crisis: African and American Opinions*, 29 June 2005, p. 3.

40 Glenn Kessler, 'Bush offers to meet with Dudan's leader to pave way for UN force in Darfur,' *Washington Post*, 30 August 2006.

41 Robert F. Worth, 'Sudan says it will accept UN–African peace force in Darfur,' *New York Times*, 17 November 2006.

42 'Sudan's Bashir denies UN Darfur force deal,' *Sudan Tribune*, 28 November 2006.

43 Glenn Kessler and Nora Boustany, 'US sets Jan. 1 deadline for Sudan to act on Darfur,' *Washington Post*, 21 November 2006.

44 Jimmy Carter, 'There's hope in Liberia's history,' *New York Times*, 13 July 2003; Princeton N. Lyman, 'How to do Liberia right,' *Washington* Post, 19 July 2003; Colum Lynch, 'Intervention in Liberia would signal shift,' *Washington Post*, 5 July 2003.

45 'Marines Withdraw to Warships,' *New York* Times, 24 August 2003.

46 US Department of State, Secretary Condoleezza Rice, 'Remarks en route Monrovia, Liberia,' 16 January 2006.

47 White House, *The National Security Strategy of the United States of America* (Washington, DC: March 2006), p. 14.

48 Nina Serafino, *The Global Peace Operations Initiative (GPOI): Background and Issues for Congress* (Washington, DC: Congressional Research Service Report RL32773, 8 February 2006), Summary and p. 5.

49 US Institute of Peace, 'Global Peace Operations Initiative: future prospects,' USIPeace Briefing, undated.

50 Testimony before the House Appropriations Subcommittee on Foreign Operations, reported in 'US mulls 75,000 strong foreign peace force,' Agence France Presse, 29 April 2004.

51 United Nations Department of Peacekeeping Operations fact sheet and data on specific operations available at <www.un.org>.

52 Serafino, *The Global Peace Operations Initiative*, pp. 4–5.

53 Ibid., pp. 6–7.

6 Threats to security

1 US Department of State, Office of Counterterrorism, 'Pan Sahel Initiative,' Press release, 7 November 2002.

2 International Crisis Group, *Islamist Terrorism in the Sahel: Fact or Fiction* (Brussels: Africa Report no. 92, 31 March 2005), p. 30.

3 US Department of State, Washington File, 'Former envoy praises Bush anti-terrorist partnerships with Africa,' 17 November 2005.

4 US Congress, House Committee on Appropriations, Subcommittee on Foreign Operations, *Foreign Operations, Export Financing, and Related Programs Appropriations Bill, 2007*, House Report 109-486 (Washington, DC: US Government Printing Office, 5 June 2006).

5 US Department of State, *Congressional Budget Justification, Foreign Operations, Fiscal Year 2007* (Washington, DC: 2006), p. 345.

6 US Department of State, Office of the Coordinator for Counterterrorism, *Country Reports on Terrorism 2004* (Washington, DC: April 2005), p. 29.

7 Ibid., p. 335.

8 Jim Garamone, 'Flintlock exercise trains Africans to handle defense,' American Forces Press Service, 17 June 2005.

9 Donna Miles, 'US increasing maritime operations in Gulf of Guinea,' American Forces Press Service, 5 July 2006.

10 Headquarters, United States European Command, 'US European Command statement following President Bush's remarks addressing global posture,' 16 August 2004.

11 Combined Joint Task Force-Horn of Africa slide presentation, September 2005, available at <www.defenselink.mil/news>.

12 'Admiral cites complexity in Horn of Africa mission,' American Forces Press Service, 24 April 2006.

13 See, for example, Eric Schmitt, 'Threats and responses: expanding US presence; US seeking new access pacts for Africa bases,' *New York Times*, 5 July 2003. 'Ungoverned areas' may be found in Statement of General James L. Jones before the Senate Foreign Relations Committee, 28 September 2005, p. 9. General Charles Wald, Jones's deputy, has affirmed that 'We cannot allow the African continent to become another Afghanistan.' Master Sergeant Bob Haskell, 'Partnering Africa,' Headquarters, United States European Command, 18 March 2005.

14 Statement before the Senate Armed Services Committee, 7 March 2006.

15 US Department of Defense, *Quadrennial Defense Review Report* (Washington, DC: 6 February 2006), pp. 33, 12.

16 White House, *The National Security Strategy of the United States of America* (Washington, DC: March 2006), p. 37.

17 Statement before the Senate Armed Services Committee, 7 March 2006, p. 9.

18 International Crisis Group, *Islamist Terrorism in the Sahel*, p. i.

19 Salima Mellah and Jean-Baptiste Rivoire, 'El Para, the Maghreb's Bin Laden,' *Le Monde Diplomatique*, February 2005.

20 International Crisis Group, *Islamist Terrorism in the Sahel*, p. i.

21 'Somalia, expanding crisis in the Horn of Africa,' Testimony by Jendayi E. Frazer, House International Relations Committee Joint Hearing, Subcommittee on Africa, Global Human Rights and International Operations, Subcommittee on International Terrorism and Nonproliferation, 29 June 2006.

22 National Public Radio interview, 26 January 2007.

23 See, for example, the BBC reports 'Al Qaeda suspect's ordeal,' 1 August 2003; 'Malawi terror suspects in Sudan,' 24 July 2003; and 'Malawi terror suspects block exile,' 23 June 2003. Also, 'Kenya terror link suspect in Zimbabwe,' *Nation* (Nairobi), 24 July 2003.

24 Craig S. Smith and Souad Mekhennet, 'Algerian tells of dark odyssey in US hands,' *New York Times*, 7 July 2006.

25 Craig Timberg, 'Mistaken entry into clan dispute led to US black eye in Somalia,' *Washington Post*, 2 July 2006.

26 International Crisis Group, *Islamist Terrorism in the Sahel*, pp. 3–25.

27 In August 2006, *Time* magazine reported that an Africa Command would be announced 'soon.' Sally B. Donnelly, 'Exclusive: Pentagon plans for an African Command,' *Time*, 24 August 2006.

28 'General said to be faulted over speeches,' *New York Times*, 20 August 2004.

29 See, for example, Paul Marshall, 'Radical Islam's move on Africa,' *Washington Post*, 16 October 2003; Ralph Peters, 'The other Jihad,' *USA Today*, 23 August 2005; Freedom House, *The Talibanization of Nigeria: Radical Islam, Extremist Sharia Law, and Religious Freedom*, available at <www.freedomhouse.org>.

30 The remark came in the wake of the discovery of an alleged terror plot in Britain to bomb airliners. 'President Bush discusses terror plot upon arrival in Wisconsin,' 10 August 2006.

31 Frederick J. Frommer, 'Senator Feingold faults Bush war language,' Associated Press, 12 September 2006.

32 The percentage figure is for 2005, while the barrel total is an average for January through September 2006. Data are from the website of the US Department of Energy, Energy Information Administration <www.eia.doe.gov>.

33 US National Intelligence Council, *Mapping Sub-Saharan Africa's Future: Conference Report* (March 2005). Available at <www.dni.gov>.

34 'Nigeria arrests "Taliban-style" rebels,' <Aljazeera.net>, 6 January 2004.

35 US Diplomatic Mission to Nigeria, 'US–Nigerian military in bilateral skills exchange training,'

Press release, 15 September 2004. According to this release, four such vessels had been delivered. A 2003 release said that seven would eventually be sent. US Diplomatic Mission to Nigeria, 'Two US government-donated ships to the Nigerian navy arrive in Lagos, 3 April 2003,' Press release, 31 March 2003.

36 World Bank, 'The Chad–Cameroon petroleum development and pipeline project: questions and answers,' available at <web.worldbank.org>. See also, Carin Zissis, 'Chad's oil troubles,' available at the Council on Foreign Relations website, <www.cfr.org>.

37 Raymond Thibodeaux, 'Anger rises in oil-rich Chad as funds don't aid the poor,' 30 April 2006.

38 World Bank press release, 14 July 2006.

39 Thomas L. Friedman, 'As energy prices rise, it's all downhill for democracy,' *New York Times*, 5 May 2006.

40 <www.eitransparency.org>.

7 Beyond the Bush administration

1 'Key judgments' of a National Intelligence Estimate (NIE) produced in April 2006 and released by the White House in September. 'Declassified key judgments of the National Intelligence Estimate on global terrorism,' *New York Times*, 27 September 2006. The remainder of the report remained classified.

2 See, for example, Admiral Gregory S. Johnson, Retired, 'The "long war" demands proactive engagement in Africa,' Center for Strategic and International Studies, *Online Africa Policy Forum* (Washington, DC: 2 October 2006). Available at <http://forums.csis.org/Africa>.

3 Global Fund, 'Pledges,' table available at <www.theglobalfund.org>.

4 Carol J. Loomis, 'Warren Buffett gives away his fortune,' *Fortune*, 25 June 2006.

5 David Remnick, 'Profiles: the wanderer,' *New Yorker*, 18 September 2006. According to Clinton, Prime Minister Denzil Douglas of St Kitts and Nevis was influential as well. 'Remarks at the XVI International AIDS Conference,' 15 August 2006. Available at <www.clintonfoundation.org>.

6 Clinton, 'Remarks at the XVI International AIDS Conference.'

7 Bethany McLean, 'The power of philanthropy,' *Fortune*, 7 September 2006.

8 Lynn Sweet, 'Next step: pressuring US on Sudan,' *Chicago Sun-Times*, 4 September 2006.

9 Lynn Sweet, 'For Kenyans, senator from Illinois has come home,' *Chicago Sun-Times*, 27 August 2006.

10 Lynn Sweet, 'Senator mobbed in Kenya, gets bribe money returned,' *Chicago Sun-Times*, 26 August 2006.

11 Joyce Mulama, 'Development-Africa: Obama to the rescue?,' Inter Press Service, 25 August 2006.

12 John C. Green, *The American Political Landscape and Religious Attitudes: A Baseline for 2004* (Washington, DC: Pew Forum on Religion and Public Life, 2004).

13 Tony Carnes, 'Jesus at G8: Christian advocacy for Africa gains notice at top meetings,' *Christianity Today*, July 2005 (Web only).

14 Green, *The American Political Landscape*.

15 Jane Lampman, 'A priority for US churches: Africa's poor,' *Christian Science Monitor*, 29 June 2005. The text of the letter is available at <www.beliefnet.com>.

16 Website of the West Angeles Church, available at <www.westa.org>. Click on 'About Bishop Blake.'

17 Website of the Congress, <www.pacec.org>.

18 The Nigeria-based Redeemed Christian Church of God, for example, has parishes in several American cities and is developing a Christian theme park in Texas. Scott Farwell, 'Africa's largest evangelical church plans a new home in rural Texas,' *Dallas Morning News*, 20 July 2005.

19 Walter Russell Mead, 'God's country?,' *Foreign Affairs* 85 (September/October 2006): 33–4.

20 Ibid., p. 39.

21 Ibid., p. 42.

22 Or as Mead puts it, 'to persuade large numbers of Americans to support the complex and counterintuitive policies that are sometimes necessary in this wicked and frustrating – or, dare one say it, fallen – world.' Ibid., p. 43.

23 Pew Forum on Religion and Public Life, *Prospects for Inter-Religious Understanding: Will Views Toward Muslims and Islam Follow Historical Trends?* (Washington, DC: 22 March 2006).

24 On Graham, see interview with Deborah Caldwell, 'A deliberate attack against the name of Jesus Christ,' available at <www.beliefnet.com>; on Robertson, 'Pat Robertson describes Islam as violent religion that wants to dominate, destroy,' Associated Press, 22 February 2002.

25 'My view of Islam,' *Covenant News*, available at <www.covenantnews.com>.

26 'China set to forge strategic partnership with Africa: Wen,' 22 June 2006. Available at Forum on China–Africa Cooperation (FOCAC) website <www.focac.org>.

27 Amnesty International, *People's Republic of China: Sustaining Conflict and Human Rights Abuses, the Flow of Arms Continues*, 12 July 2006.

28 Princeton N. Lyman, 'How to do Liberia right,' *Washington Post*, 19 July 2003.

29 Jim Fisher-Thompson, 'State's Frazer discusses US–Chinese cooperation on Africa' (US Department of State: Washington File, 6 December 2005).

30 White House, 'President Bush and President Hu of People's Republic of China participate in arrival ceremony,' 20 April 2006.

Index

Published by Zed Books and the IAI with the support of the following organizations:

Global Equity Initiative The Global Equity Initiative seeks to advance our understanding and tackle the challenges of globally inequitable development. Located at Harvard University, it has international collaborative research programmes on security, health, capabilities and philanthropy. <www.fas.harvard.edu/~acgei/>

InterAfrica Group The InterAfrica Group is the regional centre for dialogue on issues of development, democracy, conflict resolution and humanitarianism in the Horn of Africa. It was founded in 1988 and is based in Addis Ababa, and has programmes supporting democracy in Ethiopia and partnership with the African Union and IGAD. <www.sas.upenn.edu/African_Studies/ Hornet/menu_Intr_Afr.html>

International African Institute The International African Institute's principal aim is to promote scholarly understanding of Africa, notably its changing societies, cultures and languages. Founded in 1926 and based in London, it supports a range of seminars and publications including the journal *Africa*. <www.iaionthe.net>

Justice Africa Justice Africa initiates and supports African civil society activities in support of peace, justice and democracy in Africa. Founded in 1999, it has a range of activities relating to peace in the Horn of Africa, HIV/AIDS and democracy, and the African Union. <www.justiceafrica.org>

Royal African Society Now more than a hundred years old, the Royal African Society today is Britain's leading organization promoting Africa's cause. Through its journal, *African Affairs*, and by organizing meetings, discussions and other activities, the society strengthens links between Africa and Britain and encourages understanding of Africa and its relations with the rest of the world. <www.royalafricansociety.org>

Social Science Research Council The Social Science Research Council brings much needed expert knowledge to public issues. Founded in 1923 and based in New York, it brings together researchers, practitioners and policy-makers in every continent. <www.ssrc.org>

African Arguments

African Arguments is a series of short books about Africa today. Aimed at the growing number of students and general readers who want to know more about the continent, these books intend to highlight many of the longer-term strategic as well as immediate political issues confronting the African continent. They will get to the heart of why Africa is the way it is and how it is changing. The books are scholarly but engaged, substantive as well as topical.

Series editors

ALEX DE WAAL, Global Equity Initiative, Harvard University
RICHARD DOWDEN, Executive Director, Royal African Society

Titles already published

Julie Flint and Alex de Waal, *Darfur: A Short History of a Long War*
Tim Allen, *Trial Justice: The International Criminal Court and the Lord's Resistance Army*
Alex de Waal, *AIDS and Power: Why There Is No Political Crisis – Yet*
Chris Alden, *China in Africa*

Forthcoming

Mary Harper, *Getting Somalia Wrong*